The Essence of Resilience

The
Essence
of
Resilience

Stories of Triumph over Trauma

Tanya Lauer and Kathleen Parrish

Health Communications, Inc.
Deerfield Beach, Florida

www.hcibooks.com

Library of Congress Cataloging-in-Publication Data
is available through the Library of Congress

© 2016 Tanya Lauer and Kathleen Parrish

ISBN-13: 978-07573-1941-9 (Paperback)
ISBN-10: 07573-1941-6 (Paperback)
ISBN-13: 978-07573-1942-6 (ePub)
ISBN-10: 07573-1942-4 (ePub)

Publisher: Health Communications, Inc.
        3201 S.W. 15th Street
        Deerfield Beach, FL 33442–8190

Cover and interior design and formatting by Lawna Patterson Oldfield
Cover photo © iStock by Getty Images

This book is dedicated to those resilient ones
who suffered and still walk this Earth
with courage and love.

For Sallie, my mother and dearest friend:
you are the true essence of resilience and beauty.

For my dad, thank you for your belief in me.
For Noah, my heart and my joy.

For Eric, my love and my soulmate.

—Kathleen

This book is dedicated to all the
brave trauma survivors with whom I've had the
privilege of working, and to all of those suffering
with trauma who have yet to receive support.
You are not alone.

To Gabriel Ellington, Richard Lauer, Elizabeth Lauer,
and Karen Lauer: Thank you for showing me
what it means to be resilient.

To James Henry Lauer:
your light lives on.

—Tanya

Contents

INTRODUCTION

IT'S SAID THAT EVERY SCAR TELLS A STORY. However, for many trauma survivors, the poorly healed wounds of yesterday remain voiceless, their stories untold. These untold stories fester like an underground poison, eroding truth and resulting in distorted beliefs and self-blame. The trauma survivor may echo these untruths over and over and over again. *What happened to me was my fault, I deserved it. I am worthless. I am unlovable. I am a bad person. What happened to me isn't as bad as what happened to someone else.* Over time, these distortions become the story that they tell others and whisper to themselves in the deepest part of their hearts.

Sadly, many people who survive trauma remain silent about their experiences. They have learned to perfect the art of secrecy, holding the darkness of their wounds close. Perhaps they are numbly following dysfunctional family rules that prevent them from speaking of the terrible truth of their trauma. They may have learned to live with the menacing skeletons in the closet of their lives, the ancient bones rattling, threatening to expose their greatest shame. They may not ever fully recognize the way that trauma has changed their life.

WHAT IS TRAUMA?

By Kathleen Parrish

As a trauma clinician, this question has been asked of me repeatedly over the years. Just the other day, a woman spoke to me about a sexual assault that she had experienced over forty years ago. She told me that she had tried to move on with her life and that she didn't realize how much this event had affected her. She said, "I never really thought it was a big deal." As we continued to talk, she allowed the pain of her assault to surface and she cried for the first time in many years.

The truth is, she had tried, desperately and unsuccessfully, to bury that event in her past. Since then, she had been struggling with profound depression and alcoholism. Despite all of her attempts to quit drinking, she had been unable to maintain sobriety. Like so many trauma survivors, she was stuck in a cycle of self-destruction, propelling herself further into the murkiness of her shame, sadness, and anger. We talked about the aftermath of trauma—how it isn't the event itself that is damaging, but the story we tell ourselves afterward, i.e., the meaning we attach to it. So often, it's the meaning of the trauma that erodes the identity and self-perception of the trauma survivor. As a result, they are unable to see their worth, value, or strengths.

So, what is trauma? The question begs to be answered. The most accurate and formal definition of trauma is this: *experiencing, witnessing, or being confronted by an event or events that pose a threat of death, injury, or sexual violation.* In more general terms, I consider trauma to be any event that violates your sense of safety and well-being, or shatters your integrity or sense of wholeness. It's something that causes incredible sadness or a feeling of brokenness. Trauma can be isolated to one event or can be a series of events such as occurs with childhood abuse or domestic violence. Trauma can cause significant changes in a person so that they're unable to fully return to whom they were before the trauma occurred.

In simpler terms, trauma is that sudden and tragic death that you weren't prepared for, wrenching away someone that you loved more than anything. It is the assault on your body that violates your will and choice. It is that family dinner scene, the one that happened every night, where your father regularly became intoxicated and screamed at everyone. It is that constant hum of criticism and rejection that became the theme of your childhood, dished out by an angry parent. It is the parent who left you, either physically or emotionally, and never returned. Trauma is the spouse who is physically or emotionally abusive, leaving you to feel trapped and alone. Trauma can occur in so many different ways yet create the same end result: feelings of fear, anger, brokenness, sadness, confusion, and shame.

Traumatic events change people, altering their self-concept and perceptions of reality. Many trauma survivors will tell the before and after story. Before the trauma, they had hope, they could function, they could trust. After the trauma, they were forever changed. Trauma survivors often believe that trauma robbed them of everything and they spend their time desperately trying to fill the hole in their heart. Depression, self-destruction, anger, and a sense of injustice often march in the sad processional of trauma. Although many people physically survive traumatic events, they may never really live again. It's as if a part of them died in the aftermath of trauma and they flit through life like a ghost, on a haunting search for the remnants of who they were in the past, in the *before*.

While some people are able to identify the point of entry—the time and place that trauma intruded into their lives—others are left sorting through a lifetime of painful experiences with uncertainty. Many survivors experienced complex, ongoing trauma that occurred regularly during their childhood or in a relationship with another person, like a spouse. This type of trauma may be the landscape of their life, altering the way that they developed, how they viewed themselves, and how they learned to understand the world around them. Those who lived a life where trauma was an everyday occurrence may feel that their experiences blurred the lines of reality and challenged their perceptions of what is normal, what is healthy, or what is safe. As a result, they may have developed coping mechanisms that allowed them to survive. Those who live lives of trauma may become experts at reading the environment, a trait called *hypervigilance*. Always on the edge, in a heightened stage of arousal, they learn to assess perceived threats from the environment and the people around them. They often become highly attuned to the noises, gestures, tones of voice that might be predictors of impending danger. Once free of these toxic environments, these individuals often struggle to cope in healthy ways. They may gravitate toward destructive relationships or chaotic environments, finding comfort in all-too-familiar scenarios that contribute to their inevitable self-destruction. They may live lives filled with self-deprecation and shame, void of any self-compassion.

Many people who have traumatic pasts live with co-occurring disorders, such as addiction, eating disorders, depression, or anxiety. In fact, research suggests that co-occurring disorders are a likely outcome for people with post-traumatic stress disorder, or PTSD. For these individuals, the process of recovery can seem more complicated. Some individuals who experienced significant trauma may be diagnosed with a personality disorder, such as *borderline personality disorder.* Many trauma survivors lived in a constant state of danger and panic forcing them to learn skills to survive. In dysfunctional families, normal coping skills, such as expression of feelings, healthy confrontation, and individuation, are not effective. Consequently, a trauma survivor often develops skills that are more adapted to their environment to help them to survive their family system. Some of these behaviors might include dishonesty, withholding feelings, controlling behaviors, self-harm, and substance use. In my experience with co-occurring disorders, these problems speak to the devastation that trauma has caused. Trauma often shatters everything in its path. In the face of trauma, boundaries and trust are eroded and require safety, commitment, and honesty to be restored.

One of the greatest difficulties in the aftermath of trauma is living with the self-condemnation of guilt and shame. Although traumatic events are painful, it is often the belief system that develops in the wake of the trauma that cuts a path of destruction in the life of the survivor. Many people never honor what the trauma meant to them. They are lost staring at the wreckage of their lives, like victims in the aftermath of a tornado, trying to salvage something that reminds them of who they were before the storm. I often tell clients that trauma recovery requires us to derive meaning from what we survived. Finding meaning in what we survived allows room for self-compassion and gratitude. It sheds light on our resilience—that part of ourselves that refused to surrender or die. It allows us to celebrate our strengths while learning to heal our wounds.

Be advised, the stories here will be hard to read. In truth, they were hard to write. At times, you may want to put the book down and walk away. That's okay. But pick it back up again and continue reading. Although you'll read about trauma, loss, heartbreak, tragedy, and betrayal, you'll also read about the strength and determination of the beautiful survivors who are honored here within these pages. You will read about the people who fought back, who refused to quit, who forgave and overcame unspeakable horrors. Perhaps you will read about yourself in these pages and find that an ancient, painful wound has awakened once more. You may experience emotions that you thought you had buried long ago. You may feel like you are reliving a heartbreak that you have worked so hard to forget. Our expectation is that traumatic pain is often rekindled when we are reminded of familiar events that may have wounded us, whether yesterday or years ago. Keep reading to the end of the story, bearing in mind that the most painful part of any story usually occurs in the middle, never the end.

While this book is about suffering, it is also about the willingness to embrace the wounding of trauma and stand up in strength. The stories that follow are a song in the darkest of night; a song of freedom, forgiveness, and ferocity. The names and details of those found in the following pages have been changed to protect and honor confidentiality. However, the essence of their resilience shines forth. They are unforgettable individuals, filled with courage and strength. Our hope is that, if you discover yourself in these passages, you can begin to claim your own courage and strength—your resilience. Perhaps you will begin to recognize that you are unforgettable, too.

WHAT IS THE ESSENCE OF RESILIENCE?

By Tanya Lauer

What is resilience? What does it look like, feel like, sound like, or taste like? If you find it, can you later lose it, can it slip away? Sometimes resilience can seem elusive and intangible, like energy; or like a fleeting emotion, like the weather that passes through the skies. Some individuals may appear to be more impervious to stress and trauma than others. There may be times when we feel more susceptible to stress ourselves, compared to other times when we are certain of our perseverance. It may seem that some are born with resilience, like they are with good bone structure or green eyes. The truth is the essence of resilience is not available only for a select few. Resilience is not exclusive, regardless of perception. Breathing fully is an act of resilience. Reading or listening to the stories in this book is participating in openness and curiosity—both acts of resilience. In the wake of a traumatic injury, many feel like resilience is no longer within their grasp. But everyone is capable of resilience.

The experience of trauma is incredibly devastating. The impact of the blow causes wounding and leaves a permanent impact on a person. In the throes of the fight, flight, or freeze stress response the senses are heightened in preparation to ward off the impending threat. For this reason, a person in the midst of a traumatic episode experiences tremendous traction, with their senses that remain like tattoos in their hearts and minds, playing back on repeat through the reel of flashbacks, nightmares, and triggers. For example, the room where a traumatic episode occurred could be described in robust detail decades later. The textures and colors stay vibrant through visual recall; smells reminiscent of struggle and loss stay pungent and continue to infuse the survivor's olfactory senses. The haunting whisper of a perpetrator's voice, the loud boom of an explosion or fireworks, or the wailing of a siren result in a startle response and continue to assault the auditory senses. Many trauma survivors describe the taste of blood, vomit, or the taste of something beyond fear, the nausea of terror. Often the safety of touch is severed due to traumatic violation—the connection with physical comfort lost, leaving behind only the bare ache of shame and loneliness.

Because traumatic injury is felt through the senses, healing and the discovery of resilience requires a connection to a sensory experience. Beginning with the focus on breathing, trauma survivors can begin to awaken their senses in a compassionate way, reclaiming the present moment instead of feeling robbed by their painful past. In the following chapters, different practices are identified that help trauma survivors reclaim their senses, their stories, and their resilience.

The story of surviving trauma is important to share because it is effective in reducing symptoms of post-traumatic stress, in addition to vitalizing and energizing the story that continues to play out in the present. Through the story, the trauma survivor can create a safe vehicle to travel through the treacherous landscapes of their traumatic histories, and return to the present with a new understanding and perspective about their survival.

For some, there is no conscious memory of the past trauma. They have forgotten moments or even years of time, "dissociating" as a natural response in order to survive. Sharing a trauma story does not require describing explicit details of the traumatic event. Many fear reliving their traumatic experiences and do not want to feel retraumatized. For this reason, they avoid facing their pain and instead hold onto their secret, which can become toxic, and unbearable. Sharing stories of survival is one of the most important practices to cultivate resilience. This is the reason we decided to share stories in this book to clearly demonstrate how resilience was found through the narrative of survival.

A story can be shared in a myriad of ways and through many different creative mediums. Everyone has a story that may not have similar content, but shares similar emotions and themes. Often these shared experiences are of loss, of suffering, and of overcoming trauma. These themes and voices create bonds and harmonize together, creating threads and even lifelines of support and connection. We all have traumatic experiences, even if our symptoms don't meet the criteria for post-traumatic stress disorder; none of us come through our lives unscathed. Through sharing the pain and the burden of trauma with others, an unbreakable connectedness develops, community is found, and healing and resilience grows.

Over the course of the last year, as I was working on compiling chapters for this book, I experienced a blow that challenged my own concept of resilience, not only theoretically, but also personally. My father died suddenly and unexpectedly, and the way I discovered this was painful and traumatic. I remember that when I heard the word "deceased" out loud, I dropped down to the ground on my knees. Outside, in the desert, is where I heard this final news. One of the visual aspects of living in this environment is the brightness of the night sky, which is perpetually luminous and breathtaking. That night, though, held an incredible and undeniable glow. As I stared down at the ground, sick with grief and panic, I couldn't help but notice how the light reflected off the desert floor. When I looked up at the sky I was overcome with wonder. The stars were so brilliant I was reminded of my father and his love for the natural world. I felt his presence in the light that night. I still feel his presence now and his support through the process of writing this book. My father was an avid reader and spent a tremendous amount of time during his days cradling a book. He also was always in my corner, cheering me on through losses and triumphs. When I told him about the upcoming publication of this book, he responded with pride and exuberance. The reality that my father will not have the opportunity to experience the unfolding of these pages breaks my heart; he'll never have the chance to hold his daughter's book, which I know he would have loved to do. Still, the light from the stars that night remains eternal, like the love and connection that I feel with my father.

One of the reasons why I love the work that I do as a trauma therapist, and why I'm inspired to share my experiences with you as the reader, is because the stories, like mine, don't end in the darkness. When clients really engage in the truth of their survival there is so much more to the story that is unpacked and revealed. This is why trauma work is so rewarding; witnessing clients finding and owning their light and authenticity through their suffering is a profound experience that is often life-changing. This book is an attempt to honor all of the brave clients I have had the opportunity to work with. Many have spoken words for the first time, words they never thought they would have the courage to utter out loud. I have seen clients with their hands trembling, terrified and overwhelmed, but still willing to move through their fears, and open their hearts to their stories and their healing. The clients I have worked with are an incredible source of inspiration, and have shown me what the essence of resilience *really* means.

None of the following stories are one person's narrative. They are inspired by the essence of one person's resilience, or the composite of several themes of resilience, and are combinations of many traumatic themes and stories. Through the following stories survivors were able to identify natural qualities and connections within themselves that helped them to gain meaning, and transcend their profound experiences of pain. Each chapter's title, and the focus of the story, describes how this quality helped the survivor to reclaim their internal resilience. The stories are representative of the harsh reality of trauma, and include content that may be shocking, painful, and overwhelming to hear and to read. The motivation for writing this book was to portray honestly the brutality of trauma and to also describe the grace of resilience.

Many of the trauma survivors I have worked with have wanted to share their stories as an effort to support others in finding their voice, their recovery. Some of the elements of the stories and the qualities of resilience may seem familiar for you, personally, or for someone you care about or love. The hope is that these stories, although painful, may also be inspirational and relatable. Too many trauma survivors suffer in secret and in silence. My personal wish is that one reader will pick up this book and will feel less alone, and one person could be inspired enough to reach out and cross the threshold to ask for help by stepping into a meeting, or a therapist's office, or confiding in a trusted person. Sharing our stories is a healing privilege. Thanks for your willingness to join us on this journey with these brave characters and their stories. Here is to your story, your light, and your resilience.

ONE

STORY

ONE OF THE GRAVEST DANGERS OF TRAUMA is living with the wounding in silence and in secret. Often the danger of living alone with the story of trauma—hard as this may be to believe—is more threatening than the trauma itself. When a person shares the story with another, this experience offers the greatest opportunity for healing. The reason people change and leave harmful or negative behaviors is most often due to the support and inspiration of another person. Evidence-based healing happens most frequently in the context of a relationship. When a person who has felt traumatized, disenfranchised, or worthless has the opportunity to feel heard through their story, they experience transformation and discover resilience.

In the wake of trauma, survivors often feel like their story no longer belongs to them. The circumstances that caused the trauma, or the people who inflicted the wounds, become the authors of the story. The shame-based narrative that follows the suffering becomes the focus of the story. For example, if a child is abused or abandoned, then the trauma is internalized, resulting in an internal narrative like:

I deserve to be abused or abandoned.
I'm disposable; I'm damaged; I deserve pain; I'm worthless; I don't deserve to be loved or cared for; I don't matter.

Once a person believes a narrative like this, they begin to make choices in accordance with these beliefs, and the wounding continues because the power of the narrative continues.

A trauma survivor can reclaim their power by reclaiming their story. Taking the pen or the keyboard back, and deciding what the meaning of the story is for them, can change the trajectory of their future and their potential for finding their authenticity and their resilience. The story encompasses not only the infliction of the traumatic wound but also the story of healing and surviving it. The story of resilience and overcoming the trauma describes the true character of the survivor. For the abused and abandoned child, the survival narrative could shift from a shame-based narrative to one of resilience.

My parents were ill and incapable of taking care of me, but their choices were not my responsibility. It's not my choice how I was treated then, but it is my choice how I treat myself now. I am stronger because I survived abuse and abandonment. I learned that my voice matters, my creative expression matters, and I deserve to be cared for and heard. I can trust myself to share my story, and I can trust others to understand my story.

Trauma breaks us apart. Our stories bring us together. Storytelling is one of the oldest healing traditions. Storytelling is the cornerstone of psychotherapy and twelve-step recovery, and is a foundation of connection and relationship building. Since we were living in caves we have been sharing our stories to survive, heal, and understand one another. Our stories provide a bond that can tie us together, providing safety, while revealing the light of our resilience.

The practice of storytelling is intrinsically healing and provides the opposite physiological effects of stress responses. *Sharing* stories actually reduces post-traumatic stress symptoms. *Writing* our stories releases the illness from within, purging the pain and suffering onto the page. *Listening* to stories creates calm, is a natural cure for stress, and lowers our blood pressure. It's no accident that we read bedtime stories to children, as ritual, prior to their bedtime, helping them transition into a restful state and fall asleep. Sharing our stories creates healing energy, calms us, and connects us.

SHARING STORIES REDUCES PTSD SYMPTOMS. WRITING STORIES REDUCES ILLNESS AND INCREASES FEELINGS OF WELLNESS AND CONNECTION. LISTENING TO STORIES CREATES CALM.

While our stories are uniquely ours, they also capture shared experiences of our humanity, spanning time and crossing cultures. Even if the facts of our stories are different, the emotional struggle of survival is universal.

Once our stories are shared, the essence of the story transcends beyond one's person and helps energize others' stories of survival as well. When trauma survivors share their stories, what emerges is not only their pathway through suffering, but also clarification of their capacity for survival. Resilience comes through the narrative, sometimes serendipitously, but it always emerges. Trauma survivors often greet their light and their true selves through their story for the first time. When stories are heard and understood, compassion ensues—both with self and others.

As long as we are breathing, all of our stories are still alive and have potential to change course and adopt new meaning. If we are conscious of the story we are currently creating in our lives, then we have to be accountable. We have to know that our story is our legacy. Our choices influence others, creating a ripple effect that extends to all those around us, impacting their stories as well.

Often, trauma survivors feel powerless and trapped. They are also grieving devastating losses—either the loss of others, or the lost parts of themselves, like their innocence, their integrity, their ability to feel joy, or to dream. Through the story there is an opportunity to reclaim self-compassion, childlike wonder and innocence, authenticity, and hope for the future. While trauma is inherently disempowering, sharing the story of it is empowering.

After a traumatic event, many feel stuck in the past, and prisoner to the stress response they are living with. Story offers the freedom to disengage from memories and sensations of the past, and shift to focus on the present, or even on the future. Through a story we can find flow and movement, choosing a course that supports who we are, what we want and hope for, and what is healing for us.

A story can be expressed through movement, dance and art, through the written or spoken word, or through many other mediums. When stories are expressed authentically they give voice to our creativity. Sometimes there are no words for a trauma survivor to tell their story. If the trauma occurred prior to the development of language, or if there is no memory or sensory recall of trauma events, there still is a story. The body tells a story, and often when trauma survivors do not have clear data about the past, they may still have physical sensations.

One of the most painful experiences of trauma is feeling left behind, devalued, and disposed of. Even when individuals suffer horrible losses and traumatic injuries, if they have a safe and supportive embrace to fall into, this softens the blow. One of the most important indicators of resilience for children is the presence of an adult who is safe, supportive, and caring. Many clients I've worked with report that abandonment and feeling completely unworthy of love is more painful than any other experience they have endured.

In the following story the character Amanda is abandoned and horribly abused. She is adopted and adjusts to a different family, a new life, and later learns about the truth of her birth story. This information traumatizes her further, leading to the development of shame-based beliefs that result in her feeling damaged and disposable. Through her creativity and openness, she is able to articulate her story, first by writing it, and then sharing it with others. Her story brings her perspective, healing, and the support she needs. By continuing to share her story through her art and relationships, she finds compassion for herself, and learns how to open her heart with others.

"There is no greater agony than bearing
an untold story inside you."

—*Maya Angelou*

Amanda: Owning Her Story

The snow covered the usher's gloves as he fumbled for his keys to open one of the back doors of the Bolshoi Theatre on a cold, dark morning in Moscow. As he leaned into the door, frustrated and shivering, the door opened without the key. He passed over the threshold and noticed that the infrared light of the burglar alarm failed to illuminate. *Bizarre*, he thought as he continued to the office, with Russian techno music pounding through his headphones. Feeling perturbed with the night staff that allowed a security breach, he got into his uniform and put away his backpack, then settled into his work routine. These hours were uncommon for the usher's schedule at the theater. He picked up this shift to help a friend, with the hopes of running into some of the dancers during their rehearsal. He checked his reflection one last time in his phone to make sure his hair and eyebrows were on point. He smiled back, ready for another day at the theater.

As he removed his headphones a screaming sound flooded his ears and all the space around him. Shocked and startled, he checked his phone to see if something was still playing but saw the sound had been muted. He ran inside the theater, trying to chase the location of the screams. The acoustics carried the noise, which seemed to be reverberating from the front rows or possibly the stage, bouncing off the elegant gold walls of the theater. Gasping and terrified, the usher rushed toward the piercing cry. He couldn't decipher the sound; it was muffled and unclear, like it could be an infant or a wounded animal. He shuddered and listened while scanning the theater. Then he stopped short as he discovered the source of the sound: under one of the theater seats, a baby was wrapped in white blankets, red-faced and gasping for air, crying out for help.

The usher dialed emergency services immediately while his gaze remained on this helpless infant, left completely alone. He had never held a baby before but instinct drove him to cradle the tiny infant wrapped in the white blankets. The usher choked back tears, gently rocking the child and waiting for help to arrive. The baby was taken immediately to the hospital and, soon after, placed in an orphanage.

Sadly, the orphanage offered little in the way of comfort to the child, a little girl who was given the name Sasha but most commonly referred to only as her crib number. In the bleak, cold environment her cries were met with brutality, a stark contrast to the tenderness offered by the usher. The baby could have easily died at the orphanage—many there were abused, neglected, and malnourished—but instead she didn't give up struggling for air, for nourishment, and to stay alive. She was louder than the other infants, crying out frequently, and reaching with small, dimpled hands to be held and cared for. The orphanage staff grew frustrated with this baby who required so much attention, and they responded in anger, burning cigarette butts on her arms instead of holding her in theirs. They would leave her tired, hungry, and alone in the darkness.

The baby's fortunes changed one day when an American adoption agency identified the child as a possible match for a couple in the United States that was looking for a Russian girl. Her prospective parents had struggled to conceive their own child, and since they both had Russian blood in their genetic makeup, they wished for a Russian daughter to continue their cultural heritage. The abuse subsided immediately, and the baby was provided with better care and nutrition to ensure a smooth adoption process. At fifteen months old, the girl was officially adopted and renamed Amanda. Still, the lingering red scars from cigarette burns that were scattered on the inside of both of her arms held the secrets of the horror that the innocent child had endured. Her new parents knew she had been abused but accepted this as one of the conditions of the adoption process.

On the flight to her new home, Amanda's adoptive parents beamed with joy as they held her, rocking her and cherishing her like a treasure. Her appearance was similar to her adoptive mother's, and it would be natural to assume that she was her biological daughter. She looked like a porcelain doll with her light blue, luminous eyes and perfect blond curls framing her delicate face. She cried during the ascent and descent due to the pressure on her eardrums, and shrieked out during the bumps of turbulence during the flight. Other passengers may have been bothered, but her new family felt only gratitude and appreciation. They were finally holding their dream, their daughter.

Amanda didn't speak at the time she was adopted. Even with the attempts the orphanage made to cover up her mistreatment, it was obvious that she had been malnourished and met the criteria for failure to thrive. The adoption agency had shared portions of the story about how Amanda was discovered in the theater and taken to the orphanage. The report included that, due to the abuse and abandonment, there might be behavioral difficulties including mood swings and attaching to others, and also with completing developmental milestones. This information did not detour her parents' enthusiasm and instant adoration for her. They believed that, with enough love and attention, any challenges could be overcome.

In her new family home on the California coast with an ocean view, Amanda had a room of her own decorated in flowing pink with ballerina accessories, a fully equipped playroom, and doting parents who were consistently attentive and available for her. She'd smile back at them as they interacted with her at first using the sign language they'd learned in preparation for parenthood, and also verbally.

Gradually, Amanda surpassed the expectations of both her parents and doctors, and grew into a precocious toddler, becoming exceptionally verbal and expressive. Some of Amanda's fondest memories were from these years and especially around the time she entered kindergarten. She would draw and paint, sharing her art with her teachers and friends, and felt consistently celebrated. She loved coming home to her room, and watching the light of the sun glistening on the water, beyond the white and pink curtains that fluttered in front of her.

Her parents were so proud of their daughter who was flourishing and healthy and growing rapidly. They dreaded the day when they would have to share with her the story of how her life began. Behind the display of perfect parenting, they both felt anxious anticipation, constantly looking for clues of disorders, or bracing themselves for the first onset of rage, anger, or depression from their daughter. They hid the truth from Amanda about the scars on her arms and instead called them birthmarks. While they knew the truth of her birth story was important for her to understand, they wished they could wipe it away, and pretend that she was their biological daughter.

Ultimately, they decided to wait until Amanda had grown mature enough to handle and process the truth about her adoption. To them, their daughter was like a precious Fabergé egg that, if touched in the wrong spot, could shatter into many pieces. While they certainly had good intentions, in truth, withholding the information from Amanda was a way for them to avoid their own fear and anxiety.

As Amanda developed mentally, physically, and emotionally, she seemed to sense and lay claim to her place in the world. At times she sensed her parents' anxiety and discomfort but dismissed it as part of their own idiosyncrasies, or other times even thought that they were having marital problems. She rationalized these suspicions away, but still a residual question remained: was there a secret they were keeping from her? Often she'd stare at her arms and wonder why she had such unusual birthmarks, like nothing she'd ever seen on her friends. She sensed pain when she looked at them but had no coherent memory to which she could attach these sensations.

When she turned thirteen years old, her parents said that they needed to have a serious discussion. Her suspicions were correct—she knew they had been hiding something from her—and this realization left her feeling even more anxious and frightened at what they might reveal. She could never have imagined the truth and how it would affect her.

The words "adopted," and "left in a theater," hit her like a blow to the temple. Amanda couldn't focus; it was like the room turned upside down. She couldn't look at her parents and gripped the kitchen table to brace herself. The revelation only left her with more questions: "What about these scars on my arms? Are they really birthmarks?"

Both of her parents started to cry and responded, "No, you were abused in the orphanage; those are cigarette burns." Amanda couldn't hear anything else and she couldn't stay with them in that room and in that tension. She ran outside sobbing, her world became tumultuous and had turned upside down, like a ship capsized in a sudden storm. Everything she believed in had instantly disintegrated. Worst of all, her parents, the ones she loved and trusted the most, were actually liars. Her real parents didn't want her and left her, like trash, abused, branded with the scars of shame that were singed on her skin. New cognitions developed and gripped Amanda's mind. *I'm worthless, I deserve pain, I don't belong here.* With these beliefs she entered a dark depression.

The curtain closed on Amanda's idyllic scene—the exuberant and creative girl being raised in a loving home by two doting parents. Act Two was a whole new story, with the emergence of an altogether different Amanda: one who was morose and isolated, responding to her parents with barely audible monosyllabic utterances. She moved through her day in slow motion, a heavy burden draining her energy. She was consumed with ruminations about the birth parents she would never know and certainly could never understand. She thought about the people in the orphanage who hurt her; why did they do it and what was their motivation for brutalizing a baby? She felt angry about what happened, and about all the questions that would remain unanswered. Basic information that most people took for granted, she would never ascertain. What did her parents look like? Why did they abandon her? What was their cultural, genetic, and medical history? The question that Amanda kept asking herself that disturbed her the most, and kept replaying in her mind was, *What is it about me that is so disposable?*

Finding out about the adoption left her in a constant state of anxiety and discomfort. She waited for the other shoe to drop, to deal with the stinging shock of more unforeseen bad news. She hated her life and the story she was told. She rejected her body and hid under baggy clothes. Even in the heat of summer, she wore only long-sleeve shirts that she would pull down with her thumbs to conceal from the world—and herself—the scars on her arms that were a disgusting reminder of where she came from.

Other times, the pendulum would swing to the other extreme, with her disrobing and engaging in numerous meaningless sexual encounters, acting on the belief that her body was worthless and disposable. Amanda found emotional connection only through using substances, and fell in love with the cocoon of safety she created under the influence. Deepening her experience of intoxication, she combined cannabis with alcohol and then graduated to opiates. Eventually, heroin became her drug of choice; it offered her relief and gave her a joy and sense of belonging that she missed and longed for. Soon the scars on her arm were sharing space with track marks from shooting up. Amanda's story became one of addiction in an effort to drown out the feelings of hurt and rejection.

As her addiction progressed, Amanda left home and attended art school. Her relationship with her parents became remote, tepid at best. She no longer expressed anger outwardly toward them, but she struggled to trust them, or rely on them emotionally, after feeling so fundamentally deceived. She looked at her closest friends—the ones she used drugs with—as family. Sadly, one of her most constant using companions died suddenly of an overdose. Amanda tried to keep up an impervious front but started to lose trust in her safe place now; heroin, her salvation, was losing its grip on her.

Although lost and depressed, Amanda still wanted to live. One of her friends was in recovery and always raved about the inspiration she found attending Narcotics Anonymous (NA) meetings. Amanda initially felt annoyance with this friend, her collection of chips, and her constant boasting about the benefits of recovery. As time passed, however, Amanda became more curious than annoyed, though she would never reveal it outwardly. She was afraid to acknowledge the truth about her addiction and found myriad excuses to avoid crossing the threshold to actually attend her first meeting.

Once she did take that step, however, she was convinced. Amanda loved the authenticity and fellowship she experienced in the meetings. She particularly valued honesty and had a distinct aversion to anything she perceived as fake or inauthentic. This stemmed from what she saw as her parents' deception. In NA she felt like the rooms were filled with truth, and she loved hearing the stories, many of which resembled her own experience of abandonment, adoption, and strained parental relations. She wasn't ready to speak at first, but was eager for the day when she could share her story. Amanda felt embraced in the accepting atmosphere; she had been waiting to feel held for a very long time.

She found a sponsor that she liked, an artist, like herself, who was also a therapist. They became close as the sponsor guided her through the steps. Her sponsor also understood trauma, and offered to work with Amanda to help her in recovery. Her sponsor noticed how much of an impact Amanda's story made on her identity, her addictive process, and her sense of belonging in the world. She knew how difficult it was for Amanda to share in meetings. She encouraged Amanda to write down her story along with doing her twelve-step work. She explained to Amanda that her trauma and abandonment could be a significant contributing factor to her addiction.

Amanda wanted to own her story like the other NA members. Inspired by the meetings, she trusted her sponsor's recommendation. She poured out her story for the first time, and from her perspective, onto the screen of her laptop. She wanted to write it all down first before sharing out loud. It took weeks to reach the age of thirteen, and then more weeks to arrive at the present. She printed the pages out and read the words out loud as if the story belonged to someone else. Amanda was employing the mindfulness practice of *observer's mind*, which allows people to observe themselves from the outside. What arose from this objective perspective was compassion. She couldn't believe the strength it took for that little baby, herself, to cry out and survive. Once she created her story, it became powerful and meaningful, and held her like a companion. She could shift her perspective to see herself as an infant. How painful it must have been to be left for hours, beaten and burned. When she looked at her scars from the burns along with the track marks, she realized that she had been perpetrating the same kind of abuse toward herself through her addiction.

Amanda's confidence grew from the support of her sponsor and the fellowship of NA. She realized that she didn't have to internalize the negative interpretations of her worth from this story. Her birth parents' limitations in their capacity to love and care for her was not her responsibility. It wasn't her fault that she was abused in the orphanage as an innocent baby. She did nothing to illicit that kind of treatment and cruelty. Amanda dispelled the shame-based beliefs that she developed in response to the story of how she was brought into the world. She no longer felt disposable, and instead owned her talent, her value, and her authentic voice. Amanda felt a sacred energy in the story of her survival, and now when she looked at her scars, instead of shame, she saw the scars of a warrior fighting for her life, and through them openings to the light of her resilience. She no longer pulled her sleeves down to hide her arms. She didn't show them off as badges of her suffering either. She simply accepted the scars as part of her story, and had hope about the other chapters in her life that were yet to come.

Through her narrative, she developed a boundary, not only from others but from herself. As she considered how to write the next chapters in her life, she realized that she could not continue down the same destructive path she had been, causing herself pain by injecting her body with poison. To do so, she realized, was not unlike how she had been abandoned as an infant. Instead, she wanted to safeguard herself, and protect the baby—the innocent part of her that had no choice regarding how she was treated. Now Amanda did have a choice, and she could no longer participate in the pattern of self-sabotage.

Amanda worked hard with her sponsor on the ownership of her story, and her choices in her recovery. While she was initially angry at her adoptive parents for withholding the truth about her early years, she understood in therapy that what she felt was shock and confusion, that what she had known as her life was really just covering up the reality. She realized that her birth story was traumatic for them to share with her as well, and she developed more understanding for why they avoided telling her the truth for so long. Amanda acknowledged that her shock and anger at finding out the truth could have been feeding the beast of addiction that had taken hold of her. She reached out to her parents, let go of any residual bitterness, and developed an honest and loving relationship in her recovery. She could now feel the gratitude she never felt before for their choice to adopt her. Through her story Amanda could understand how much she appreciated their desire to love her, care for her, and provide her with a home. As Amanda grew more compassionate for herself, she could also feel compassion for stories of others.

By finally being able to open up about her past, Amanda's connection with others deepened, not only with her sponsor, but also her friends in the NA fellowship and in the local art community. She now celebrated the opportunity to share her story in meetings and in any other setting where her narrative could be beneficial for herself or for others. In recovery, her artwork developed and bloomed. Now she found different ways to share her story of survival, not only through words but also through her paintings. She released the expressions of her heart into her canvases, and felt such release and pride in her work, regardless of how her work was received.

There was an audience for Amanda's paintings, and her work was shown and sold through several galleries in her hometown, as well as nationally. Amanda loved to listen to others' stories and also to engage in them through their art. One of her favorite pastimes was meandering through the various art galleries in her area, getting to know the owners and also spending considerable time observing other artists' paintings. She felt connected with their stories through their work, and tried to absorb and understand their experiences.

A gallery owner named Edward, who frequently hosted showings for Amanda, took a special interest in her and in her work. She spent many mornings in his gallery talking about art, what inspired her, and what inspired other artists. Edward was an artist himself and could understand Amanda's story and language, almost like it was reminiscent of his own. He had suffered and survived childhood trauma as well and, through therapy and through the expression of his art, he found healing. Amanda loved to listen to his story and the soft, gentleness of his voice. Their relationship had been a deep friendship for months now, but was progressing toward an even deeper intimacy as they found themselves spending hours together. They spent hours in her studio listening and sharing their stories, her paintings surrounding them, and the white sheets that covered her work wrapped around the two of them.

Amanda learned from her trusted sponsor that she should be careful with intimacy. She explained that this space between emotional and physical intimacy was slippery for Amanda because of her trauma and attachment issues. In recovery Amanda had developed very firm boundaries and had avoided intimate relationships for a long time to really focus on her own healing. She didn't want anyone to come between herself and the recovery she worked so hard to build and embody. Amanda knew she wanted to let go and trust again, but now there was more at stake, much more to risk.

One day, as she considered all of this, Edward touched the scars on her arms joining his identity, his fingerprint, with the depth of her pain. No one before embraced this part of her. She stayed in this moment uncertain of what would unfold. She knew that part of her was still like the baby alone in the theater, reaching out and crying to be held. Through her story, Amanda found a way to hold and cherish herself. In doing so she created an opening and a freedom to be held by others. She exhaled, released, and embraced this moment.

~

TWO

SOURCE

BECOMING RESILIENT OFTEN MEANS TRAVELING: being willing to voyage toward a treacherous place that pulsates with pain. The destination is usually hidden away in the darkness, in the depths of our hearts and minds, and it is the source of our wounding. Before the decision is made to take this journey, there must be contingencies established, considerable planning, and plenty of patience. There are no maps and no guarantees; the destination can change and morph into something different, requiring unexpected detours. Having a trusted companion for support and guidance can help the traveler arrive safely. This guide can also offer resources and assurance for a safe return home. The choice to go to this destination and encounter the trauma is a brave one, one that many never attempt. For those who are willing and ready to explore the depths of their source of pain, resilience awaits them on the shore.

The Greek root of the word trauma is *trōma,* or wound. Sometimes, wounds are very visible and impact functioning and mobility in a very physical way. For some, psychological wounding can be more difficult to detect. Often the wounds are insidious and tucked away, sometimes only surfacing under stress. For others, the echoes from the source of pain cry out, haunting survivors with constant reminders of the hurt and terror of the past.

The solution for many is to drown out the wounded source with alcohol or other chemicals in an attempt to numb and bring relief. Unfortunately, drug use and addiction may provide temporary relief but will exacerbate and further infect the wound in the end. Many others turn to other afflictions, fixating on food, either on consumption or restriction, or on people, becoming eclipsed in others in a codependent fashion, or isolating to avoid the potential of further injury. They develop elaborate avoidance strategies, often unconsciously, in the effort not to feel or get lost in the darkness of the source of their pain.

Many believe that they are weak or even the opposite of resilient if they are affected by trauma, or the ancient chapters of their lives. Common messages—from other people or even from within—can sound off in a way that may be well-intentioned but feel dismissive and belittling. Messages like: *Get over it. Don't let it bother you. You should be past it by now. Forget it and move on. There is nothing you can do about it now.*

We are all wounded in different ways and for different reasons. There is no expiration date for how long trauma impacts a person. In my experience as a trauma therapist, wounding has lifelong effects unless the wounded is treated, attended to, and addressed. Development often stalls during a traumatic injury. A part of a person remains emotionally the age of when the trauma occurred. To find resilience, it often takes going back to this age, imagining the younger part of the self that was wounded, holding that innocence, and integrating the pain with compassion. When a person chooses to reach out and face the fear, unexpected opportunities arise, opening the potential for healing. The source of pain transforms into something different, something less frightening and more luminous.

The irony is that when a person faces their pain safely and with support, there is relief and reward. Sometimes this is a protracted process. Much like cleaning out a physical wound from an injury, the process can be very painful at first. Many clients I have worked with have expressed tremendous gratitude for finding the courage in themselves to share their story of trauma. I have frequently heard statements like these:

I wish I shared this twenty years ago; it was scary at first but now I'm so relieved. Now I don't feel like this will affect my wife/husband/ children so much.

I feel like a burden has been lifted.

It's not my fault. Sharing this secret has changed my life, I am free . . .

When trauma survivors face their fears the power and intensity of the source diffuses. Often, what trauma survivors see instead is the light within themselves that was there all along. Going to the source becomes a spiritual passage of tolerating ambiguity and walking through fear. Many grow in confidence after they take this journey, and develop an awareness about how to face the darkness of trauma in the future. They understand that within them is the strength to overcome, and they learn that they can find their light and resilience no matter what obstacles they may face in the future.

The following story is about Henry, a very brave and resilient man who suffered living with a painful secret from his childhood that he tried to bury for many years. Until he had the courage to disclose the source of his pain, he struggled. Even with the most disciplined and valiant efforts, he could barely breathe or live with himself. Once he had the courage, with the support he needed to tell the truth, he was released from the internal prison of shame in which he had been trapped. Through sharing his story, Henry found the resilient light within himself that gave him hope and meaning, and he created a life that he could be proud of, one of authenticity and honor.

The cave you fear to enter holds the treasure you seek.

—*Joseph Campbell*

Henry: Unearthing the Source of His Pain

Henry was a young adult, only eighteen, but seemed like a throw-back from another time—much older than his chronological age, cautious and discreet, with a modern gentility. Other men tried to emulate his style, and women swooned over the soft glide of his voice and the gentle grace of his gestures. He had acquired a steely, solid work ethic and a velvet charm. But Henry's outward orderly appearance was a stark contrast to the tumultuous terrain of his internal landscape. He never spoke about his childhood trauma; instead he kept it buried and hoped that he would die with this secret sealed within him. The source of his pain was like an untreated wound that continued to throb and remind him of his past.

Henry exhaled with relief as he transitioned into adulthood. He embraced his independence and finally felt emancipated from the past. He could decide what his destiny would be, and he could shape his identity into the person that he would be proud of, instead of feeling ashamed of who he was. No one knew the other side of Henry, the traumatized part of him that felt constantly confused, disgusted, and filled with self-hatred. He was determined to leave these feelings behind and tried desperately to hide any remnants of the past. Still, memories would surface unexpectedly. The smell of sweat flooded Henry with revulsion and nausea. The sound of a diesel engine approaching would trigger Henry, throwing him back in time emotionally, sending him into a high state of alarm and anxiety. Although he was a six-foot-tall, muscular man, these triggers would immediately turn him back into a small, helpless child with nowhere to turn.

"The few, the proud, and the brave" was the emblematic Marine slogan that Henry wanted to represent. As a child he would whisper the words to himself, imagining buttoning up the gold buttons on the navy blue uniform of an officer. He knew he would become a Marine, and he believed that this was the answer to quiet the questions and insecurities that kept him restless and distraught throughout his days and nights. Henry envisioned the uniform as a kind of shield, offering protection from these sensations, making him capable of defending himself, and becoming impenetrable to the fear and violation. Relaxing and trusting enough to sleep had never been easy for Henry. During the day, he felt mostly in control; he'd utilized techniques that worked reasonably well in a conscious state. At night, however, his stress level spiked, and he was constantly haunted by nightmares. While most people look forward to the rest and renewal that sleep provides, Henry hated it because it made him feel out of control and powerless. He would start his days by waking up shaking and sweating. He would immediately run to the shower, and turn the water on to the hottest temperature he could tolerate in a sort of emotional and psychological catharsis, as though the cascade of scalding water would sanitize and wash away the horrible feelings that plagued him for so long.

Although Henry sought military service and would pledge to defend our country, in reality he was already fighting a war, one within himself, battling the feelings and sensations of the past and the aching source of his pain: the shame from the dark secret that he could not quiet or defeat. No matter how much he tried, Henry was beginning to realize he was losing this ongoing battle. The enemy Henry was fighting was much more insidious than any that he would fight in the Marines, for it was invisible and ever-present. There was no dignity in fighting this menace. Dying did not scare him. Instead, the thought of death was a welcome respite from the struggle and the trauma that tethered him. Henry achieved his goal and became a Marine, and shortly after was deployed to Iraq and then Afghanistan. Becoming a Marine was everything he hoped for and Henry felt eager for combat. The discipline, goals, and rituals kept his trauma symptoms temporarily at bay. Being a Marine gave him a strong, honorable identity, and offered him a sense of purpose, clarity, and camaraderie. The Marine Corps became a new family, and he developed bonds and felt profound loyalty to his fellow Marines. Henry knew that the likelihood of facing another traumatic experience in combat was extremely high, yet ironically, he welcomed this possibility and quietly hoped that it would overshadow his memories from his youth. During his second deployment in Afghanistan, Henry and his best friend and fellow Marine were alone in a building when a bomb detonated, the blast throwing both of them out into the street. Henry survived, but his friend died instantly from the impact of the explosion. The last image Henry had of his friend was the vision of his distorted face covered in blood, and his mangled, unrecognizable body, lifeless on the concrete.

Henry had survived many brushes with injury and death before, and would die for his friends if necessary. Henry often would take the riskiest missions, priming himself to make this sacrifice. As the medics carried Henry away, lifting him into the helicopter, his chest ached with pain and sadness, along with a strong sense of anger with the lack of justice in this outcome. As he said good-bye to his friend and brother, he wished he could have taken his place. He would have been freed from his trauma and given a valiant ending to his own story. To die in combat as a Marine would be sudden and clean, a way to depart this world with honor. While Henry missed his friend, he secretly wished to join him, or find a similar exit strategy for himself.

When Henry returned home from "the Sandbox," military jargon for Afghanistan, he tried to develop a plan to guard himself from the emotional stress of his numerous traumatic experiences. Part of his plan for living "back on the block" (stateside), included enrolling in college courses, and the other part entailed the consumption of vast amounts of alcohol. He drank socially and casually before in a controlled way; the alcohol was effective in dampening his stress and curbing his inhibitions. Now he wanted to immerse himself in drunkenness. Drinking worked to wash out the flashbacks of his childhood and of Afghanistan, at least temporarily. Henry started to isolate due to the level of intoxication that he now required. With a few exceptions, alcohol became his constant companion. He no longer socialized outside of his apartment, and would delete messages and contacts instead of responding like he used to do with wit and enthusiasm. Henry's charm had not completely departed, and he mustered up the energy to have the occasional drunken one-night stand. Drinking and sporadic sexual encounters only offered fleeting relief, and he knew that he was circling down into an abyss of darkness and alcoholism.

As the months wore on, Henry lived in a swirl of afflictions, heavy depression, post-traumatic stress disorder, and alcoholism. Even when he drank at dawn to avoid waking moments of sobriety, the dread still crept in. He was running out of options. He frequently considered committing suicide, and he had the means, his guns, and a clear plan to complete the mission. Henry wanted it to be over. He was done with the fear, done with the disgust about the past. Even with his uniform on, he no longer felt like a man.

What stopped Henry from pulling the trigger, even when he came so close that he held the barrel of his gun to his temple, was honor. He knew this choice would dishonor his legacy, devastate his family, and disappoint his other family, the Marine Corps. He could not pull the trigger, even in the most desperate moments, because he knew in his heart that this was not how he wanted his story to end.

During a routine medical check at the Veterans Affairs hospital he denied having suicidal ideation, but he couldn't hide the acuity of his alcoholism, which was flagged by his primary-care physician. He was referred to an addictions group and a trauma therapy group. Henry was reluctant to follow the recommendation because he never believed that talking and crying in a group would change his circumstances. He much preferred an intoxicated one-night stand with a voluptuous woman to console himself, rather than sitting in a circle with a group of depressed alcoholics. The deeper truth was that he feared that somehow, if he opened up and really trusted someone in a therapeutic setting, the secret he had been hiding for so long would emerge. He couldn't afford to put himself in a position of vulnerability.

Henry's integrity and sense of duty to fulfill his obligations, even in the depths of his darkness, drove him to show up for his first group meeting in the VA basement. As soon as he set foot in the room, he wanted to turn around and run back out the door. Staying for the complete group session required incredible patience. Henry couldn't focus, felt tremendous anxiety, and couldn't wait to get his hands on a drink. Group members were mature and welcoming, and appeared comfortable sharing their stories and giving each other support and feedback. The group therapist, Stan, sat in his chair carefully listening and nodding for most of the hour. He was dishevelled, wearing a crumpled sweater that looked older than Henry, fogged-up glasses, and shoes that looked like they'd never been shined. This person did not represent trust or guidance, and definitely lacked the understanding of the discipline it took to be a Marine. Henry knew that his judgment was extremely superficial—a defense mechanism born out of fear—and justification for reasons not to "trust the process," as the other group members chanted frequently in unison. Underneath all of the judgment of Stan, Henry trembled with fear.

After the group session, Henry blacked out from drinking. He woke up sick, tired, and overwhelmed. It felt like a gravitational pull was drawing him closer to the whole truth of his story and the source of his pain. Exhaustion and surrender were beginning to set in for Henry. Constantly scrambling to cover up his secret all these years took an enormous amount of energy, and he had been continuously barraged by the stream of trauma symptoms. He realized that if he was going to survive he had to try something different—he had nothing left to lose. It was time for Henry to summon up his courage again as he had done so many times before. Instead of avoiding this dark shadow that followed him everywhere, this time he was ready to turn around and face it, but he knew he couldn't do it alone. That day he called Stan and asked to schedule individual therapy sessions.

Henry told Stan that there were some secrets he wanted to disclose that had kept him a prisoner of trauma and alcohol, and he could only do it one on one.

When Henry arrived for his session, he viewed Stan with a less critical lens. His glasses looked like they had been cleaned and Henry noticed his socks were well coordinated and popped with considerable style. Maybe he had it together after all, and was more trustworthy than Henry gave him credit for. The first few sessions were focused on learning how to begin a sober lifestyle. Henry became curious about the benefits of recovery and began opening up about parts of his story. He shared some of the trauma he experienced in Afghanistan and the loss of his best friend. Henry never expected therapy to work like this. He felt like a burden had been unloaded every time he shared a part of his story, and he liked the feeling of talking to a person who seemed stable and steady, a person who wouldn't hurt or abandon him. Henry started to invite Stan into his story—sharing more of his experiences with more depth and honesty instead of hiding behind his defenses—and as he shared more chapters of his life, he exhaled more deeply.

Henry stuck with the sessions, and as the months went by an amazing thing happened: Henry began to trust himself and started to develop trust in someone else for the first time. Henry realized that while he had judged Stan harshly, Stan had never demonstrated judgment or condescension toward him. Instead, Stan expressed openness, understanding, and compassion. Even the way Stan looked at Henry felt safe. Stan became a great teacher and mirror of acceptance, and Henry began to realize how he had been suffering through his judgmental vision of others. He grew to realize that judgment was a defense mechanism that created a barrier for intimacy with himself and others that was dangerous; living alone with the shame of his secret was like a toxin that was killing him.

Henry decided to take the risk to let down some of his defenses; he had faith that on the other side of the walls was something different, something new to live for. After several months of weekly therapy sessions, Henry was ready to go to the source and share his secret. He trusted that Stan's compassion and presence would guide the way. He walked into Stan's office, hands shaking, his legs quaking to the point that he barely made it to his chair. Unable to look Stan in the eye, he said, "I have something I need to tell you and I don't want to talk more about it today, I just want to get it out. I've never said it out loud before." Henry wanted to race out of the room, forget the whole thing, and get a drink and swallow all this tension down. Deep down he knew that wasn't the answer. He had worked hard for his first few months of his recovery, and the strategy of escaping into alcohol never worked before. His hands kept shaking and he stared at the floor. Stan didn't speak, but Henry could hear him breathing calmly and patiently. Henry tried to focus on his own breathing, a new technique that he was learning.

They sat there in silence with only the sounds of their breaths audible, and their exhales eventually synchronized. For the first time, Henry did not feel alone. Time passed. He wasn't sure how much, but he wasn't giving up. He knew he could do this. He spoke, and out came the words he had held in for so long.

"I could stand walking over my best friend's dead body, it was awful but it made sense. That's not the reason why I feel disgusting every day, why I drink, and why I wanted to die. I was sexually abused when I was a kid." He couldn't remember what Stan said next but he was done. His legs were shaking now. He got up and said, "I'm done for now. I have to go." Stan walked him to the door, his voice trailing off in Henry's ear, something about recommendations for safety and their next session.

Henry left the room but had to lean against the hallway walls for support because his legs kept buckling underneath him. He'd staggered like this before, but it was always because he was intoxicated. This time was different. He was shocked with a charge of wakefulness, as though he'd been sleeping through his life up until now. For the first time he didn't want to drink. This unfamiliar feeling was raw and pure. Revealing the secret made it lose some of its potency and power over him. Henry had just purged something that had been gripping him for so long. As he stumbled through the halls he felt a paradox of instability and freedom. He felt a deep pride like he had just gone through "the wall" while running a race, his legs cramping beneath him, but he knew he was breaking through and getting ready to cross a finish line that previously felt like an impossible achievement. By speaking the truth, he knew his life had just been altered.

Henry continued to attend therapy while counting his days of sobriety. Together they traveled through the painful experiences of Henry's childhood. Henry spoke about how much he loved his mother and how he treasured time spent with her, because it was so infrequent. She worked two, sometimes three jobs with several different uniforms. Henry would give her massages in the mornings after overnight shifts, and he would help her launder her uniforms in between her different jobs. Henry realized why his Marine uniform had meant so much to him, because it represented structure, order, and connection with his mother.

He never knew his father, Henry told Stan. He had one picture and he'd received several cryptic phone calls from the man who was supposedly his dad, but had never been a true father figure in his life. Later, his mother told him that his father was an alcoholic who refused to change, and wasn't interested in taking any responsibility for parenting. Stan explained how Henry was genetically predisposed to alcoholism due to his family history. This helped Henry to perceive himself differently; instead of an alcoholic failure, he began to see his condition as a disease. As Henry continued to accumulate days of sobriety, he grew feelings of pride about his recovery and understood that addiction didn't have to be his destiny.

Henry explained to Stan that he'd had to fend for himself as child since his father was not present and his mother had to work tirelessly to support them. Henry's mother started dating a man when Henry was around seven years old. The boyfriend had earned a significant income, though Henry never understood how, and he dripped with symbols of wealth. He drove a luxury car with a diesel engine, and when he pulled up to their apartment Henry and his mother felt like they had been rescued. Her boyfriend helped his mother pay for expenses during the next five years, and provided them with new electronics—TVs and video game consoles with the latest games— and groceries. He purchased whole new wardrobes for Henry and his mother, who were both overwhelmed with gratitude for his generosity. Still, Henry's mother continued to work several jobs, and she warned Henry that her boyfriend had a dark side: he could be moody and unpredictable, and everything could change quickly.

His mother's boyfriend was nice and funny, and Henry appreciated his help. He would come over in the afternoons and evenings when Henry's mother was working, and they would watch movies and play video games together. Then everything changed. The

boyfriend started touching him, which left Henry shocked and confused. He felt indebted to the man and he wanted his approval. He
felt disgusted about what was happening but didn't understand what
sexual encounters meant and wanted to trust him since he was his
mother's boyfriend. Henry felt like he couldn't say no. As he shared
his story with Stan he realized that this was when he started hiding
his secret, when he began feeling ashamed, and when he lost his
voice.

The abuse continued for five years, until Henry turned twelve.
He'd grown stronger, was maturing, understood his sexuality, and
decided to spend less time at home in his mother's apartment. His
mother's boyfriend stopped paying for the rent and providing for
Henry and his mother, and left town. Henry's mother was distraught,
and she'd become accustomed to the lifestyle her boyfriend provided;
she became angry and resentful about their current circumstances.
While she hadn't completely trusted her boyfriend, she nevertheless
turned a blind eye to anything that might have forced her to do something about it. As a result, Henry spent the rest of his adolescence
and teen years with friends, often even staying at their houses. They
lived on the edge of high-risk behaviors. Henry drank alcohol but
never used any other drugs and would never break laws. Even then he
dreamed of becoming a Marine and refused to take part in anything
that could jeopardize this goal.

One part of Henry's story that he never understood before he
was in therapy was his relationship with his mother. He loved her
but also felt confusion and anger about the circumstances with her
boyfriend. Henry and his mother lost the emotional connection they
shared when he was a young child once her boyfriend became a part
of their lives. Henry sometimes wondered if his mother knew about

the sexual abuse, but either denied or pretended that it wasn't happening because they needed the financial help. Confronting him could have jeopardized this arrangement. Henry remembered trying to give his mother clues about the abuse, and he thought for a while she had to suspect something, but she never took action, which broke Henry's heart more than he was aware of. He felt betrayed by his mother, like she didn't protect him when he really needed her. In his discussions with Stan, Henry became aware of all of his feelings, even if some were in conflict with each other. He loved his mother, and he also felt hurt by her; both feelings were true. Stan helped him find the insight regarding the connection between his childhood trauma and his adult intimate relationships. Physical and sexual intimacy were not a problem, but the fear of betrayal and lack of trust prevented Henry from feeling any emotional intimacy.

While sharing his story Henry cried more than he had ever cried before in his life. Stan comforted Henry with his consistent nods of understanding and approval. Stan explained how much shame Henry had internalized due to the violation, along with the lack of protection he felt from his mother. Stan described how children are like sponges and absorb everything emotionally, and take on the responsibility for the adults around them. Henry could see how he had been living with this burden of shame, how he felt so disgusting about being touched inappropriately, and how worthless he felt because he didn't know how to stop it. Together, Stan and Henry visualized that Henry could travel back to the seven-year-old part of himself, trapped in that apartment. He could take that seven-year-old out of there, hold him, and tell him it wasn't his fault.

Over time, Henry came to understand and truly believe that the abuse was never his fault. He began to feel more compassion for himself, and started to unlock more of his emotions instead of hiding behind a wall of repression and control. Some of the new emotions that emerged spontaneously were the feelings of joy and hope for the future. He felt open to possibilities, new dreams, and understanding for the child part of himself that had been fighting to survive for so long.

Eleven years after the day when Henry shared his secret with Stan, he leaned back in his soft leather chair, exhaling with contentment. The space he created was beautiful and comfortable in keeping with his stylish aesthetic. His socks always popped to punctuate his looks as an ode to Stan. It wasn't just the chair or the external trappings that brought Henry peace. His life had become his own story, and he felt pride and compassion for what he had achieved. He found his own exit strategy from suffering and it wasn't suicide; it was sharing the traumatic source of his story and finding honor in surviving it. It had been eleven years since he'd picked up a drink, felt disgusted with himself, or considered suicide. Challenges continued; there were occasional knocks of trauma symptoms and depressive episodes, but a great burden had been lifted. He enrolled in college and completed a doctorate in psychology specializing in post-traumatic stress disorder. After Henry's life had so drastically changed in those moments with Stan, he decided that he wanted to be a catalyst to support change for others. Henry knew that many other veterans were suffering and suicide rates were high. He could understand their pain, and knew that many veterans were also survivors of childhood trauma. He believed he could help them find the truth about their own identity and story. His work as a therapist was much like his service as a Marine. There was purpose and honor in serving and supporting his clients. Henry continued to breathe deeply as he considered the significance of this day, and waited for his last session to arrive. Afterward he would return home to his wife and two daughters, who had his favorite red velvet cake waiting. Tonight his family would celebrate his sobriety birthday: the day he came back to life.

~

THREE

VOICE

AT TIMES, WE'VE ALL FORFEITED our right to speak for ourselves. Perhaps we were being polite and didn't voice our concerns at the office meeting. Maybe we withheld our opinion about a friend's choices because we didn't want to hurt their feelings. On occasion we may decide that it is more important to listen than to speak. However, when this unwillingness to voice our thoughts or feelings is a pattern of behavior, it can result in dysfunctional relationships, depression, anxiety, anger, and self-destruction.

Our voice and our willingness to use it are two of the most powerful resources available to us. Our voice provides us with the ability to protect ourselves, to define ourselves, to advocate for ourselves, and to allow us to have authentic and meaningful relationships with other people. Our voice is a reflection of who we are and an expression of our unique experiences. Our voice is an advocate for ourselves and for others. Our voice is the steady heartbeat of our emotional existence and our fiercest protector and supporter. If we learn to use our voice appropriately, we can experience safety, peace, and well-being, even in the midst of difficulties.

Sadly, many trauma survivors have lost the ability to use their voice. Often, they're silenced by painful events that have caused heartbreak and a crushing loss of self-esteem. Over time, repeated traumatic events can change beliefs about self and cause survivors to question their worth and value. Many trauma survivors believe that they will not be heard or supported. They may feel as though they do not have a right to speak for themselves or fear that their needs will never be met. They may spend their lives allowing other people to speak for them.

They may not even recognize their own authentic voice. Often, trauma survivors become detached from their bodies, minds, and emotions. They may have difficulty understanding what they truly think, feel, want, or need. As a result, they walk through life mute and unable to express even the most basic truths about themselves.

Recovery from trauma requires that the survivor learns to find and use their voice. It is essential that they learn to identify and express emotions that may have long been ignored or denied. They may need to experience validation of their pain and suffering. They may also need to develop an emotional vocabulary—a way of understanding and speaking about their emotions—that has previously been undeveloped or underdeveloped. Recovery provides survivors an opportunity to identify, express, and honor their pain. It allows them to recognize their right to feelings, and needs that they may have spent a lifetime denying or minimizing. It also allows them to establish boundaries and structure in relationships, and situations that ensure continued safety. It allows them to understand and embrace their unique perspectives on the world around them. This process fosters self-compassion and self-respect, the two necessary components of sustained recovery.

Finding our voice requires courage and a willingness to feel very uncomfortable. At times we may feel selfish or demanding. We may experience fear of rejection or believe that our needs will never be met. We may long to return to old behavior patterns that helped us feel more secure. Using our authentic voice will allow us to understand and meet our own needs, rather than leaving us to depend upon others to read our minds or fully comprehend us. It supports us to walk in a life of recovery and authenticity where we can experience safety and true intimacy with those who love and support us.

"The privilege of a lifetime is to become
who you truly are."

—*C. J. Jung*

Melissa: Finding Her Voice

Any outsider would conclude that Melissa led a charmed life. She came from a wealthy family and everything she needed and wanted was always right at her fingertips. She lived in an elegantly decorated, luxurious English country estate that boasted ten bedrooms. She had a stunning view of a meadow from her bedroom window, where she could watch her father and his friends as they organized on the lawn for a fox hunt. In the spring, the countryside surrounding her home was filled with flowers, sunshine, and promise.

Melissa was a baby when her parents employed a nanny to care for her. When Melissa was two years old, her brother Michael was born. Three years later, their little sister, Kathryn, was born. Her siblings were sweet children, although at times they were a bit unruly. Michael was an adventurous soul who enjoyed tree climbing and collecting wayward frogs who had hopped into his path. He seemed to stay dirty and was often playfully chided by the nanny, who seemed to be enchanted by his mischievous grin and penchant for charm. Kathryn was an adorable girl—a tiny blond—who loved to be the center of attention and was the apple of their father's eye. She was often requested to make an appearance at her parents' dinner parties, where she would be perfectly comfortable making her acquaintance with utter strangers. She would dance or sing for them, delighting the guests who found her to be fairy-like in her features and mannerisms.

Melissa realized that she could never be in the spotlight like her sister. And because she was such a serious child, she lacked her brother's spirit of adventure. Throughout her childhood, she remained quiet and nonintrusive. She simply sat, watching the world go by, wishing for connection yet unable to find the intimacy she so hungrily desired. She often felt like a misfit in her family, as though she had been dropped in among them by some alien force. When she was very young, she began to wonder if she had been adopted or switched at birth. She would squeeze her eyes shut and imagine that her real parents would ring the doorbell, swoop in, and proclaim her their child. They would want to hear everything she had to say and they would hold her close while they told her they loved her. But when Melissa opened her eyes, all she saw were the well-adorned walls around her and the long shadows cast on the fine furnishings of her home.

As a young girl, Melissa learned what was expected of her by her parents and those around her. She was taught that she should not speak unless spoken to, she exhibited graceful table manners, and said please and thank you at the required times. Although Melissa was a quiet child, she longed to feel important to someone, especially her mother and father. She often felt like one of the many pieces of elegant silver adorning the display cases in her house: polished and refined, but not really of any practical value. And like the silver, Melissa learned to keep her flaws hidden—to only allow others to see those things in her that were considered praiseworthy. Melissa knew that others envied her family's wealth and that they saw only the polished parts of her family. Melissa knew that they could not see the emptiness that swelled inside of her with a fierceness that threatened to overtake her.

Melissa accepted her life, but often thought that she might not have chosen it for herself had she been given the option. Although ensconced in surroundings that sparkled and gleamed, she often felt alone and invisible to others. Melissa wanted a simpler life. She longed for the love and care of parents who asked about her school work or took time to take walks with her in the glorious sunshine. Melissa envied her friends who lived in more modest houses, whose parents worked traditional jobs. Unlike Melissa, they had never known how nannies filled the day with structure and routines. They would never understand the looming threat of boarding school, something that had been decided long ago for Melissa. She envied the warmth and caring that she saw amidst relationships between her friends and their parents. She felt the polite exchanges she received from her parents were merely counterfeit forms of love, poor substitutes for the real thing.

As Melissa grew older, she learned more about the complexities that governed her family. As a barrister, Melissa's father was a very powerful man who was both highly respected and greatly feared. Melissa was keenly aware of his anger, and she worked hard to keep his temper at bay by being compliant and polite. Although her father was never physically violent, she knew of his capacity to turn silent and cold. She learned to avoid his steely gaze, which always seemed to be appraising her for some indicator of betrayal or misbehavior. At times, his gaze would survey her body, and he would launch into a lecture about the importance of being thin and keeping the body in good condition. Melissa would turn her downcast eye toward her mother and notice her skinny, model-like appearance. Later, alone in her room, Melissa would look at her body in the full-length mirror, her skinny legs and too-big feet, and would promise herself that she would never be fat. She allowed herself to hope that this might be a way to gain her father's approval.

Melissa learned early on that she could not rely on her mother for support or guidance. Although she was well-intended, she was absent in her role at home. She often had a vacant stare and seemed distracted by obligations or commitments to local charities or organizations. Melissa longed to sit with her mother while she readied for a meeting, if only to watch her brush her golden brown hair and adorn her neck with the delicate, antique pearl necklace that had once belonged to her grandmother. Melissa wanted to be powerful like her father, and beautiful and thin like her mother. But mostly, she wanted her parents to notice her and be proud of her. She wished she could call out to them and tell them that she needed them. But her voice fell silent in the face of their power and importance.

At the age of eight, Melissa was sent to a boarding school where she was thrust into a new world, far from her home with the lovely view of the meadow. She had always been a quiet child but now withdrew even further into herself amidst the clamor of other boarders who seemed to stare at her and whisper. Melissa hated boarding school and begged to return home. Her pleas were met with polite and empty reassurances from her parents, telling her that she would adjust to this new life. They reminded her that they had enjoyed boarding school and that it would provide her with the best education. They told her that she was expected to excel and that her feelings of anxiety didn't make sense.

In spite of her parents' directives and assurances, Melissa battled fierce anxiety, one that twisted her gut and left her feeling paralyzed.

She carried this anxiety with her everywhere she went, like a cruel host that dictated her life. At times, her anxiety was so intense that she felt like she couldn't breathe. It seemed worse at mealtimes where she worried incessantly about gaining weight. She remembered her father's lectures about staying thin and she would critically examine her body at every opportunity. She began to skip meals when she could and would hide in the bathroom until she was sure the dinner hour had ended.

As time passed, something dark and painful began to emerge within Melissa. Like the subtle changing of seasons, Melissa blossomed into adolescence, typically a time of great angst and confusion. Melissa's mood seemed to change frequently, and she would find herself suddenly feeling angry, irritable, or sad for no particular reason. She had grown taller and more angular in her features. She had a heightened awareness of her body and worried about others' opinions of her.

Melissa noticed something else about her body, something that made her feel a little bit elated—she had lost weight. Strangely, this also brought her an immense sense of relief. She felt a surge of power when she looked at her body in the mirror. She liked the way her hip bones jutted out from her small frame and she would finger them lightly for reassurance. She knew that other girls were talking about her, about how skinny she was, but she dismissed their chatter. She would stare at them defiantly from under her mascaraed eyes and dare them to confront her. She told herself that they were jealous of her because she stayed skinny where their bodies had become more soft and curvy. Even though Melissa had become a frequent subject of discussion among her peers, she hoped she would not attract the attention of her teachers or the school staff.

In a rare twist of circumstances, Melissa now feared that her parents would notice her or try to interfere with her life and her body. On visits home, she would don large, baggy sweaters and loose-fitting pants to cover her bony frame. At mealtimes with her parents, she would push food around on her plate while occasionally nibbling on a bite of vegetable to give the appearance that she had eaten while not really eating much at all. She felt anxious as her father's gaze traveled the length of her nearly emaciated figure, and felt a growing anxiety when he remained quiet. She was relieved to return to school after a weekend visit home. At school, she could stay in her room and disappear into a book, living for a while in a fantasy world where her heart didn't hurt so much.

It wasn't until Melissa's weight dropped to eighty-seven pounds that anyone expressed concern about her. It was a fellow boarder who reported her weight loss to the headmaster, who had summoned a nurse to examine her. Melissa felt a mixture of terror and anger when she was called to the nurse's office on a warm spring afternoon. By this time, she was worried about herself and her inability to stop starving herself. In school, they had learned about addiction and Melissa believed she was addicted to losing weight. She was weak, depressed, and strangely obsessive. She no longer really craved food and she noticed that she couldn't really eat anymore. Her once thick hair had become thin and patchy. Her menstrual cycle, which began at age fourteen, had disappeared. She had dark circles under her bulging eyes and she noticed an unusual flutter in her chest. She was scared and confused. She wanted desperately to be seen and to be invisible at the same time.

Melissa sat in her underwear and bra while the nurse examined her body, asking questions about her calorie intake and eating habits.

The nurse tried to hide the look of concern on her face, but she seemed alarmed by Melissa's condition. She jotted down notes in a chart and made Melissa stand on a scale backward, so she couldn't see her own weight. Melissa heard her gasp as the numbers on the scale revealed themselves and she quickly scribbled them down. She asked Melissa to get dressed and then walked her to the headmaster's office.

Sitting in the headmaster's office, Melissa was filled with a sense of fear and shame. She cried silently to herself as the headmaster asked her the same questions that she had answered for the nurse: how long have you been losing weight? Are you unhappy? Why did you do this to yourself? The last question sent Melissa reeling: *how long have you been doing this to yourself?* For such a long time Melissa believed that her self-starvation was a gift; it was a way to gain approval and to find some control in her out-of-control life. She truly believed that she would stop if she could lose just a few more pounds. Later, Melissa was asked to sit in the hallway outside the headmaster's office while her parents were contacted. She was being asked to leave school for medical care and treatment of *anorexia nervosa*.

The next year of Melissa's life became a blur as she stumbled from physicians and hospitals to a long-term eating-disorder treatment center in the United States. It was a struggle for her to allow others to fully see and understand how far she had deteriorated. Her greatest source of shame came from seeing the look of disgust on her parents' faces on the day they came to retrieve her from the boarding school. They didn't speak to her directly when they arrived that day. They spent a few hours talking with the headmaster and the nurse, listening to recommendations and concerns. Melissa sat out in the hallway waiting for them to emerge, like a prisoner waiting to learn of her sentence. In the end, her parents walked out of the school quietly, sniffing indignantly as she trotted behind them, keeping her head low and her eyes on the ground in front of her.

Melissa had been at home for a week before her parents spoke to her directly. During that time, the nanny, who had been like a surrogate mother to Melissa, was directed to inform her of doctor's appointments and psychiatric evaluations. Melissa sat in her bedroom during this time with a tray of food placed in front of her by the housekeeper. The housekeeper stood for a while, watching as Melissa made the pretense of eating, shuffling her food around on her plate as a distraction. As soon as the housekeeper left the room, Melissa promptly flushed the remaining food down the toilet. At the end of the week, she was examined by a physician who specialized in treating eating disorders. With a grave seriousness, he recommended that she be hospitalized immediately.

Later, at the hospital, Melissa was horrified to learn that she would be fed through a nasal gastric tube. She felt humiliated and alone, wishing that someone would talk with her—*really talk with her*. Her parents dropped her off and did not return again until it was time for her discharge nearly one month later. Melissa understood the message they were sending: she had disappointed them and had caused her family shame. She felt as though she were dead to them now. In moments of quiet reflection, she realized that she'd felt that way for a very long time.

Melissa endured the punishing silence of her home, waiting for the consequences to be meted out by her angry and stoic parents. They came together that day, her father on a rare day off from his job, dressed in their elegant clothes. They sat tentatively in their chairs and explained that they were sending her away to get well. As they spoke, they looked around the room and at one another, but they didn't look directly at her. Her father reminded her that this was all for the best and that he hoped she could return and finish school. Melissa cried silently as they spoke but did nothing to protest their decision. She realized that a part of her wanted to go away from them, from their cold and calloused expectations. She wanted to go somewhere that she could be seen and heard. She wanted to be somewhere with people who believed that she mattered.

During the following ten months, Melissa worked hard at her recovery. Although gaining weight was very difficult for her, she was experiencing her life in a different way. She was learning so much about herself and was beginning to understand why her eating disorder had become so powerful. At times, she was tempted to go back to that life, especially when her old clothes became too tight to wear and the scale indicated that she had gained a few more pounds. Like clockwork, she would find herself feeling anxious and she would feel a strong desire to restrict her food intake or to count the number of calories in her meals. She felt some regret when she could no long finger her hipbones or see the ridged edge of her collarbone under her shirt. When these old thoughts or behaviors would flare, Melissa put herself in the trusted hands of her therapist and her doctors at her treatment program. It was with great skill and compassion that they would help her find her way back again.

Melissa's parents came to visit and participated in a family therapy session. During the first session with her family and therapist, her father made note of her weight gain and expressed concerns about her getting fat. Melissa held her breath. Her first instinct was to cry, then to run. She felt herself sitting rigid in her seat, like a scared animal. In the most kind and gentle manner, her therapist placed a hand quietly on Melissa's arm as if to remind her to breathe and to wait before acting on her impulse to run. Melissa took a long time to breathe, keeping her head up and her eyes facing forward. Once she had collected herself, she did something she never thought she would do—she confronted her father. She spoke to him directly and firmly, sharing her thoughts and feelings with him about his comment and about the way in which he viewed her. When she was finished, she felt her hands shaking and placed them quietly in her lap, determined that he not see her fear.

As far as Melissa could remember, that family session with her father was the first time that she had ever expressed anger toward anyone. It was the first time that she allowed herself to say what she needed or wanted. All of her life, Melissa wanted to be seen by others without ever actually seeing herself. She had stuffed so much anger and resentment down into her body that it needed a release valve, and it had found one in her eating disorder. During her time in treatment, Melissa learned how much of her eating disorder had been about the anger of invisibility. She had tried for so long to be invisible that she had nearly disappeared. Ultimately, Melissa knew that her survival would depend on her ability to use her voice, her most powerful advocate and wisest friend.

~

FOUR

TRUST

THE WORD *TRUST* IS OFTEN OVERUSED. By definition, trust means a firm belief in the reliability, truth, ability, or strength of someone or something. We say things like "I trust you had a good weekend," "I trust that the account is in good shape." But trust is something more than just an acknowledgment; it is a wholehearted belief in something. Trust implies the ability to allow ourselves to cast off doubt and surrender to something or someone without reservation. Although we say we trust others, we may struggle to offer our complete trust.

By nature, children are more trusting than adults. Children trust so easily and allow themselves to be vulnerable and open to those around them without hesitation. This tendency is often worrisome to parents who fear that their children might fall prey to someone who could violate that trust. Children have an innocence about them that prevents them from understanding their vulnerabilities. They may have difficulty comprehending the concept of evil or betrayal because they have never experienced anything like it. They have powerful beliefs about the ways in which good overcomes all evil. They have magical, trusting, and beautiful hearts.

Sadly, by the time we reach adulthood, we learn about mistrust. We learn this by being hurt, betrayed, or abandoned by people to whom we offered our complete loyalty and devotion. Afterward, in those moments of raw awareness, we vow to guard our hearts more closely and not be so gullible. When we are traumatized and wounded deeply and often, we may also learn to believe that we cannot trust ourselves either. This inability to trust ourselves may develop when we are very little. The childhood filter of egocentricity can often leave us blaming ourselves for those painful wounds. We may tell ourselves that what happened was something that we could have prevented, or changed, or stopped. We may nurture a childlike belief that we were somehow in control of what happened to us. We may despise our vulnerability and our willingness to trust others so openly. These may become the focus of our mistrust of self.

When we experience trauma, we may lose our ability to fully trust ourselves or others. Our struggle to trust may leave us feeling suspicious, vulnerable, or afraid. We may look for reasons to mistrust someone or sabotage relationships that could potentially offer us the intimacy and love that we so desperately crave. Renewing trust in self and others is a gradual process and requires support from those around us. Trusting others does not imply that everyone deserves your trust. It means that we can trust in small steps at a time, while evaluating the safety of relationships. Are your friendships defined by honesty, loyalty, kindness, and respect? If so, move forward and allow yourself to develop greater levels of trust. If relationships are defined by anger, suspicion, betrayal, and confusion, then trust and intimacy are not deserved. It is okay to be careful when caution is indicated. Not everyone will earn the right to be in your life.

In the process of reestablishing trust, you will make mistakes. You will be afraid and you will question yourself. You will also be required to forgive others. Sometimes, people we love will unintentionally make mistakes that hurt us. We need to be prepared to accept apologies to allow for healing in relationships. Be prepared to feel uncomfortable, vulnerable, and afraid. This is a healthy response to new behavior. The product of mistrust is loneliness, suspicion, and anger. The product of healthy, trusting relationships with others is love and connection. We have the power to choose the emotional quality of our lives and our relationships.

"We're never so vulnerable than when we trust someone—but paradoxically, if we cannot trust, neither can we find love or joy."

—*Walter Anderson*

Jim: Learning to Trust Again

Sometimes we struggle with the things we have seen, the images haunting us and flitting just around the edges of our conscious mind like a phantom from another realm. We shake our heads, we rub our eyes, and we try to convince ourselves that we are okay. But often the traumatic images are seared into our brain with an inescapable permanency. Despite our best attempts, we struggle to understand how we survived the nightmare of that day, that hour, that moment when our life was turned upside down. For Jim, it was the eyes of his father that haunted his dreams and awakenings. He saw those eyes every day, everywhere he looked.

Jim loved his father, despite his abusive and unpredictable behavior. Although others knew his father as a troubled man, Jim tried to see the best in him. Like many trauma survivors, Jim was fiercely loyal to his dad, in spite of the many times that he had hurt or betrayed him. Jim often blamed himself for his father's anger and believed that he could change the way his father felt or behaved toward him. Jim tried hard to be helpful at home and to be a good student, hoping to make his father proud. His father's rapid mood swings made it difficult for those around him to predict his next move. For Jim, it was like being trapped on a frightening roller coaster ride with sudden drops and turns, and no seat belt or lap bar to keep him safe.

Throughout Jim's early childhood, his father was flighty, impulsive, and self-centered. He placed his own needs and wants above those of Jim and his younger brother. His father would go off on lengthy tangents about politics or religion, holding the family hostage until he finished his rambling tirade. Other times, his father's eyes would become vacant and he'd be filled with an inexplicable rage as he destroyed furniture or smashed windows. After those particularly dark times of anger, his father would sweep into the house, eyes alight with joy, and would shower the family with extravagant gifts as he proclaimed his love and adoration for them. To Jim, these rare occasions of generosity and warmth blotted out all the pain his father caused. He would lock onto his father's eyes and feel connected to him once again.

As Jim grew older, he recognized that his father's eyes were a barometer, foretelling what was to come. Those eyes could predict calm times or the coming of a dangerous storm. Jim learned that if he could accurately gauge his father's mood, then he could avert some of the fallout caused by his father's explosive rage. Despite the fear he felt for his father, Jim also felt something else, a form of admiration for his complexities. He thought of his father as powerful and in control of those around him. Jim trusted his father to win over the darkness that threatened to destroy him, and subsequently, the entire family. He believed his father would be an example for him of struggling and overcoming. Sadly, Jim's father would only leave his family with a legacy of pain and confusion.

When Jim was fourteen, his father went missing. He left to put gas in the car and didn't return. After three days, when he still hadn't shown up, Jim, his mother, and brother notified police. They checked his father's favorite hangouts and called around to friends and neighbors. No one had seen his father anywhere. Jim tried to remain positive but couldn't shake the nagging feeling in his chest that something was really wrong. Where could his father be? He knew his father wouldn't just leave. Jim felt despondent, afraid, and powerless. He wanted to believe that his father would emerge through the front door of their house, having finally conquered his demons. Jim sat on the staircase that faced the front door and waited. As soon as he came home from school he'd resume his silent vigil from the steps. More than ever, he believed his dad would come home. He wanted to look into his eyes and connect with him. He wanted to tell him that it would be okay, that everyone struggles, that he forgave him.

In the evening of the fifth day, after what seemed like an eternity, Jim saw headlights in the front yard. He jumped from the stairs where he sat and ran to look out the window. He saw his father's familiar silhouette climbing from the car. His father closed the car door and began walking, slump-shouldered, toward the house, carrying a container. Jim's heart raced as he threw open the door and shouted greetings to his father as he approached. His father walked toward him, staring blankly, as if he didn't know him. Jim's excitement drained and was quickly replaced by a steely, cold fear in the pit of his stomach. His father's eyes were not dark, they were just empty, as if washed of color and life. Jim stepped back to allow his dad in the house. He tried to make eye contact but his father was robotic and blank. In his hand, he carried a gas can.

Jim's mother and brother ran into the living room just as his father walked in. They were both crying and his mother began to fire questions at his father. "Where have you been? Don't you know how worried we were about you? Why did you leave? What . . ." She stopped mid-sentence as she saw his empty eyes and the can of gasoline in his hand. She knew, they all knew, that something was terribly wrong.

What happened next was a moment so terrible that Jim can hardly speak about it without anguish. He doesn't remember the exact sequence of events, but he remembers the look of his father's eyes as he lay dying on the floor, having consumed the contents of the empty gas can lying next to him. He remembers his mother's shrieks and cries. He remembers his brother's silence. He remembers the lights of the ambulance, arriving too late. Jim cannot recall every detail because trauma is often not remembered sequentially or rationally. What is often recorded in memory are the horrifying sights, sounds, smells, and feelings. What tortures Jim the most is the unshakeable memory of his father's eyes: pleading, taunting, sad, and strangely satisfied.

Jim stumbled through the days ahead, numb with grief and shock. His young mind, ripe with the capacity for magical thinking, kept expecting his father to wake up and return to them. He knew that something powerful and strange had taken his father away from them. Although part of him felt relief that his father could no longer hurt them, he also felt incredible confusion and sadness. He wanted to believe that it was not too late to fix things and bring his father back. But his father was dead, and he was not coming back. In the years to follow, Jim's confusion, sadness, and anger evolved into a form of darkness and depression that would pull at him.

As an adult, Jim lived a life that was absent of purpose or meaning. He often felt robotic and disconnected. He had no significant relationships outside of his mother and brother. Jim worked as a graphic designer but did not enjoy his job. His coworkers thought of him as an odd man, albeit brilliant. Jim ate poorly and often appeared disheveled. He eyes often seemed vacant, devoid of any awareness of life around him. His lips were constantly chapped and cracked. Although this feature was disturbing to those who knew him, he didn't seem to notice. When people spoke to him, they were often forced to look away from his mouth. It was as if Jim had vacated his body long ago, and he was impervious to his own physical pain or needs.

When Jim wasn't at work, he would don a pale yellow sweater over his baggy, shapeless pants. The sweater had belonged to Jim's father and Jim wore it to feel connected to him, as a way to remember the good parts about him. When he closed his eyes and smelled the sweater, he believed that he could still smell traces of his father's aftershave. Jim refused to wash the sweater, fearing he might wash away any evidence that his father ever existed. In many ways, the sweater was the one remaining link he had to his father. In spite of his father's abuse and violence, Jim held on to the tiny bits of kindness his father had bestowed upon him—the lavish gifts he gave or the infrequent buoyancy of his moods. These fleeting memories often came with feelings of confusion and sadness. Jim struggled with the belief that his father truly had some goodness within him. In many ways, Jim's adult struggle was reflective of his childlike need to find hope in the midst of darkness. Like a fairy tale, Jim wanted to believe that this story had a happy ending. He wanted to believe that all fathers love their children, and protect them from harm and danger. This was the essence of Jim's struggle; he was grieving for the father he never knew, the father who could protect him and provide for him. In many ways, he was still waiting for this version of his father to show up and take care of him. As an adult, Jim spent his days in isolation and loneliness, fearing to trust others and unable to trust himself.

On most days, Jim ate lunch at the park by himself. With downcast eyes, he sat on the same park bench, eating the same lunch of a ham and cheese sandwich. He drank lukewarm coffee from his father's thermos, now a faded gray and garnished with a few minor dents. He chewed his food as he stared at the ground, unaware of the birds singing their songs of spring, or the blades of grass peeking their heads out of the earth beneath his feet. Every day, Jim would finish his lunch and walk, in melancholic somnolence, to his office on the fifth floor at 201 Market Street.

On one particular day, a cool spring breeze caught his attention and caused him to look up briefly from his sandwich. As he glanced up, he noticed a woman sitting on an opposite bench across the side-walk from him. Normally, he would look away from people, not wanting them to see him or to analyze the pain he felt was obvious in his eyes. But today, he rested his gaze on her face, his eyes finding hers. To his surprise, she smiled at him. He felt flustered and embarrassed by being seen, but strangely, he felt himself smile back at her. She waved shyly at him, wiggling just the tips of her fingers. He looked around, unsure of what to do, having such little human contact in his life. He waved back in return, an awkward gesture, and quickly looked down. He felt flustered and unsure as he gathered the remnants of his lunch into his lunch box, stood quickly, and walked away. His heart was pounding and his face felt flushed and hot. He felt embarrassed as his legs carried him out of the park and toward his office. As he neared his building, he realized that he was smiling, something he had not done in many, many years.

In the days that followed, Jim found himself looking forward to his lunch hour. He quickly walked the few blocks to the park in hopes of seeing her. As he scanned the area, his heart would flutter and a small surge of joy would rush over him when he would see her perched on her bench. He became more courageous every day, and he would find himself initiating a wave or a smile. She seemed equally happy to see him and she would eagerly wave back. He couldn't believe how happy he felt to see her and to have that small interaction with her every day. Jim felt like something was changing in him, as though something inside of him was waking up after a very long sleep.

On one particular day, Jim was surprised to find her bench empty. He felt sad and disappointed. He was worried about the woman and hoped she was okay. Even though they had never spoken a word, he felt a strange kinship with her—a connection that went beyond words. As he sat staring at the ground, he was unaware of the sound of someone approaching.

"Hello, I thought I would introduce myself. My name is Emily." Jim nearly fell off the bench. He glanced to his right and saw her sitting beside him, her blue eyes watching him.

For a moment, he couldn't find his voice. He stumbled on his words, and then cleared his throat. "I'm Jim, how nice to meet you." His voice sounded foreign to his ears as he extended his hand in a formal handshake. Her hand was warm and soft, and Jim realized that this was the first physical contact he had experienced since his childhood. He could feel her kindness and humanity thawing the icy pain in his heart. It broke through the barriers of his sadness and longing. In those few seconds, Jim allowed his heart to open, and he felt a sense of trust—something he hadn't allowed himself to feel since his father died.

In the weeks that followed, Jim found himself thinking less about his father's death and more about how his father's death affected him. He realized that his father's passing left him rudderless and afraid. He had trusted his father to guide him and stay with him throughout his life. Instead, he had spent all of those years alone, unwilling to trust others and unable to trust himself. But his friendship with Emily had opened up something within him and he longed for more. He knew he needed to let go of his father but he didn't know how.

One day, at the local coffee shop, Jim spotted a flyer on the community bulletin board. Amid the notices about lost dogs and music lessons he spotted an advertisement for a grief support group. Jim almost laughed as he imagined himself sitting in a group of people, crying about his father. He turned away from the bulletin board and walked to a nearby chair to wait for his coffee order. But he kept turning the idea of this group over in his head. *Would it help? Could I do it?* Could he trust other people to be the keepers of his story?

Jim's order was ready and he picked it up and walked toward the door. Just as he was about to walk out onto the street, he turned around and went back into the coffee shop. He went to the bulletin board and quickly jotted down the address and times of the grief group. His heart was racing and his thoughts were conflicted. On the way back to work he had a curious feeling of hope in his heart.

The grief support group was held in a small conference room at a local synagogue. Jim found it easily enough but loitered outside the doorway, lost in a debate with himself. He felt weak and needy, unlike the person he had been since his father died. He had been stoic and unfeeling, an impenetrable wall of apathy. But now the ache in his heart, the one he had buried so long ago, emerged from the rubble of his loss with a quiet clarity. This broken heart belonged to him and it was time to claim it and mend it.

The group was different than Jim imagined. He feared it might be a group of older ladies talking about their late husbands. Instead, the group was composed of people of all ages and from all walks of life. As Jim listened, he began to recognize the universality of grief—the way it robs you, changes you, and breaks you. Jim told his story that night, too. Instead of feeling judged or misunderstood, he felt supported. What started as a group of strangers was now a group of friends and fellow sojourners.

As Jim told his story, he began to understand his grief more completely. He wept openly for the father that he never really had and realized how often he longed for a real father, someone who would be a tower of strength in the midst of life's storms. In turn, Jim could appreciate his own strengths that helped him to survive his childhood. He began to understand that his father had suffered from an illness, something that was powerful and destructive, plaguing him with sadness and eroding his willingness to live. Jim recognized his father's fragility and released himself from the responsibility he felt for his father's behavior. Jim allowed himself to feel compassion for himself as a small boy, who only wanted to be loved and protected. He also embraced the flicker of compassion he felt for his father, who suffered and died.

As time passed, Jim was able to banish the memory of his father's eyes as he lay dying. As a child, he believed that those eyes told a story or held the answer to his father's irrevocable decision to leave him. But as he searched his heart, he knew that his father's eyes were a reflection of his suffering and pain. Those eyes reflected his father's battle to live and his painful decision to die. Jim began to let the memory of his father's eyes go as he took in more of what was around him now—the love and friendship of beautiful people who saw his value and worth and wanted to share life with him.

Jim's recovery was now reflected in the way he let other people into his heart and life. It was also reflected in the way he cared for himself.

He was able to look in the mirror and see himself for the first time in many years. He began to recognize what he needed and how to provide for himself. He put away his father's yellow sweater—not yet ready to throw it away—and learned to find comfort in people and the simple art of self-compassion.

Jim continued his journey through his grief, and at the same time, watched his friendship with Emily blossom. They were the two ends of his story. Saying good-bye to someone for whom he felt both love and fear, and opening his heart to someone new. He could say good-bye to his father and still hold on to the beauty of his existence without being tortured by memories of his erratic life and his agonizing death. In doing so, he could fully embrace being loved and loving in return. His heart had been waiting patiently for this moment. He was worth it.

~

FIVE

RESPONSIBILITY

RESPONSIBILITY IS AN IMPORTANT ASPECT OF MATURITY. We are taught to take responsibility for our actions. We strive to follow through with our commitments and to acknowledge and learn from our mistakes. We take responsibility for the damage to relationships when we have knowingly or unknowingly wronged other people. Most people are able to accomplish this developmental task without much difficulty. However, trauma survivors may struggle with an altered belief that they are responsible for events or the actions of others. This type of self-blame is directly related to an inability to stop or control past traumatic events that left them feeling helpless or damaged.

Trauma survivors often blame themselves for painful events in their past. They mistakenly believe that they caused their own pain and suffering, or that they could have prevented the trauma from occurring in the first place. This type of belief system can result in codependent patterns of behavior that often reflect attempts to control outcomes or people. As a result, trauma survivors may engage in relationships with people who are unhealthy or who struggle with self-destructive behaviors. The trauma survivor may assume responsibility for rescuing or controlling these people, even to the determent of their own lives, often leaving the trauma survivor feeling lonely, angry, empty, and sad. They may engage in substance use or struggle with depression or anxiety.

In the same way, trauma survivors must begin to let go of guilt or shame for the suffering of others. Often, they can be traumatized when they assume that they are responsible for or could have prevented someone else's pain. Sometimes, they can experience trauma through another person's suffering, such as a parent, sibling, or beloved friend or partner. This type of *secondary* or *vicarious trauma* occurs when we witness, experience, or learn about how trauma has impacted someone else. Trauma, whether experienced directly or indirectly, can result in changes to our behavior and our beliefs. It can cause us to take responsibility for things that are out of our control while forsaking our own need for care, support, and safety.

Recovery from trauma often requires that the trauma survivor begin to establish the truest sense of responsibility: for one's self. This means that the survivor must begin to put their own needs above the needs of others and that they must evaluate relationships and establish guidelines for safety, trust, and accountability. It requires that the survivor allow other people to struggle and sometimes fail. Although a painful process, it is necessary to support healthy relationship patterns whereby everyone takes responsibility for their own behavior, no matter how difficult.

Recovery allows us to honor the sadness of others and to respect their ability to overcome hardships. It is a process that supports others to grow from their pain and to recognize their own strengths, without being rescued prematurely. Often we are so uncomfortable with a friend or loved one's struggles that we try to pull them away from their source of pain without allowing them to find their own way. When we do this, we are communicating a belief that we see them as powerless and weak. In turn, they often begin to see themselves in the same way. Allowing others to struggle through pain and foster resilience promotes healthy boundaries and a true sense of responsibility for self and others.

> "One's philosophy is not best expressed in words;
> it is expressed in the choices one makes . . . and the
> choices we make are ultimately our responsibility."
>
> —*Eleanor Roosevelt*

Naomi: Responsible to Herself

Her large brown eyes are soulful and compelling, playing curiously against the sharp angles of her face. This gives Naomi a mysterious appearance—an exotic combination of cunning and wisdom. Her short brown hair curves just below her jawline and is carefully styled to reveal her long neck. She stands a mere four feet, eleven inches, and is lithe and lean, muscular and fragile at the same time. She speaks with wisdom but clings desperately to those around her, like a frightened child who is terrified of abandonment. At times, she is confrontational and bold, yet other times she is avoidant and fearful. Those around her find her to be a walking contradiction and are often confused by her. If the truth were known, people would discover that Naomi feels confused about herself, too. She's perplexed and frightened by her brokenness and she can't seem to find a remedy.

Naomi feels like two different people. The Naomi who lives on the inside is childlike, anxious, and sad. Mostly, though, she is guilty—for wanting more when she has enough, for not being grateful, for complaining, and for living when others have died. She realizes that these are unusual things for her to feel guilty about, but she is unable to shake the feeling. Guilt wraps itself around her heart and mind with a sickening grip and suffocates her will, her choices, her freedom.

In stark contrast, Naomi's outside persona is fiercely defiant, feckless, and brazen. She has a history of failed relationships with men, all of whom seemed to be as tortured as she. Despite a profound sense of loneliness, Naomi continues to ignite relationships with men whom she knows are incapable of understanding or loving her. Even though she longs to feel whole, she continually shatters herself against people who are as broken as she feels—*inside and outside.*

Naomi was born in 1946 to parents who were Polish immigrants. Her parents relocated to the United States from the Polish city of Lublin three years before Naomi was born. Although they tried desperately to create a new life in the United States, they continued to be pulled back to the life they knew before Naomi was born. This other life had a name, one that seemed to have changed her parents forever: *Majdanek*. It was a strange word that seemed to carry emotions with it—painful emotions like fear, anger, and sadness. Her father's voice would become husky and choked when he uttered the word, like he wanted to purge it from his body. Sometimes, her father would be angry and would shout the word as though by sheer defiance he might conquer the horrible meaning of it. Other times, her father would become fearful—paranoid even—and would forbid the family to leave the house. He seemed convinced that someone was watching them, documenting their movements. Naomi lived in a constant state of fear for herself and for her family. It was like something dark and menacing was lurking just beyond the edges of reality, waiting to destroy them.

Naomi's mother seemed to live with a different set of scars than her father. A critical and disapproving woman, her mother habitually pointed out all of Naomi's shortcomings: "You are ungrateful. Why should you have it so good when others are suffering? You are too fat! You eat too much when others starve. In Majdanek, people would have been grateful for crumbs. You are too stupid. People will certainly take advantage of one like you. You are so matronly, why would any man want to marry you?" These and other such criticisms became the theme of Naomi's childhood. She found herself working hard to please her mother, only to fail each and every time. Her sense of shame grew as did a belief that she was a great disappointment to her parents. Although she didn't yet understand the significance of Majdanek, Naomi knew that somehow that word had caused her parents a great deal of suffering.

Time has a way of revealing things unspoken and, in time, Naomi learned about her parents' past—why they lived with the steely cold knife of fear in their hearts. When she was eleven, Naomi learned that her parents had survived the Holocaust, and imprisonment in Majdanek, a concentration camp located on the outskirts of the Polish city of Lublin. Naomi felt a deep sense of sorrow and guilt when she understood the degree to which her parents suffered. She realized that she lived a life much different than her parents had ever known. She felt greedy and gluttonous, but mostly, she felt responsible. She began to believe that she was as guilty as those who had caused her parents so much pain in the dark and torturous yesterday of Majdanek.

She learned that her parents had been arrested, dragged from their home, and imprisoned in separate sections of the camp. They spent several months in Majdanek, each wondering and not knowing if the other was alive. As days turned to weeks, their fear grew as rumors of people that were killed began to filter through the emaciated and frightened group. The soldiers were cruel and punishing, beating and berating the imprisoned. They were often deprived of sleep and then forced to work for many days without relief. They lived in squalid conditions in the camp, which was infested with rodents, lice, and disease. They went days at a time without food or water or were forced to eat slop not fit for a farm animal. On the coldest of days, they were forced to march in ice and snow for endless hours with minimal clothing. Many of those imprisoned did not survive. Sadly, Naomi learned that her aunt and uncle were also prisoners in Majdanek. They did not survive. They were among the many casualties of the heartless Nazi regime.

The more that Naomi learned, the more she felt sorry for her parents. She felt sad to think about her father and all his fears and anxiety. She could also forgive her mother for her constant anger—why she set such high standards for Naomi to reach. Naomi believed that her mother wanted her to have a different life, one in which she could be safe, happy, and loved. Naomi's mother and father never offered her love or kindness, not in the ways that most people would expect. So, Naomi became an interpreter of their actions: seeing love in their anger, kindness in their harshness, protection in their criticism. Naomi became determined to make them proud, even though a part of her knew that they would never express pride in her. She felt like an empty vessel, waiting for them to fill her with love and acceptance. She felt hungry and lonely, and hovered near them, always expectant.

Naomi carried a picture in her mind of whom she wanted to be. She believed that, if she could somehow be the perfect daughter, she could ease the memory of her parents' experiences. She thought she could show her parents that she was the reason why they had survived such atrocities. If she could achieve greatness then their suffering had meaning. If she were perfect, then perhaps she could mend their broken hearts, erase their terrible memories, and heal the wounds of Majdanek. Unfortunately, Naomi's own festering wounds would ultimately stand in the way of her success.

In high school, Naomi was a star student, excelling in advanced placement classes and graduating magna cum laude. She was captain of the debate team, a star basketball player, and student body president. She was wildly popular, had a series of very attractive boyfriends, and was invited to every single party and social event. Naomi learned how to carry herself with confidence, how to assert herself, and how to navigate the difficult social waters of her large network of friends. Everyone who knew her believed she was a shining star; no one ever saw a glimpse of her inner persona. On the outside, she was bold, beautiful, and successful. On the inside, however, she was crumbling and afraid.

Despite her early accomplishments, Naomi was plagued by the belief that she was undeserving of success. And it seemed that no matter her achievements, her parents would turn their faces away in disgust or displeasure. It was as though they understood her obvious need for their attention, her aching desperation, and they were disgusted by it. In their eyes, Naomi always felt like a needy, incompetent child rather than the intelligent, young adult that she had become. In the face of all her successes, she believed that she perpetually fell short of the love and acceptance she so desperately craved. Over time, Naomi began to give up on her quest to gain her parents' approval. It wasn't a conscious decision, but rather a recognition that she was too vulnerable, and that this weakness was a flaw that could be repaired neither by success nor accomplishment.

Over time, Naomi began to falter. Her initial missteps weren't obvious to others; they seemed only to be mere variances from her normal self. She was accepted to study at Stanford and moved away from home. She lived in a dorm, went to parties, and enjoyed the attention of various young men. Despite the university's rigorous academic program, she studied less than she did in high school, and when her grades failed as a result, her reaction was more apathy than concern. She began to receive notices about academic probation, which she threw away in defiance and disgust. Those closest to her whispered about how she was no longer a big fish in a little pond, but just another average smart girl who may not be smart enough to make it through freshman year, let alone to graduation at Stanford. Naomi dismissed the whispered judgments, knowing that her failure was already imminent, like the coming of a storm.

As the school year progressed, Naomi's stumbles became more evident. She was failing and unable to turn things around. The old fear of disappointing her parents began to roar in her ears, and she made a hasty decision to drop out of school. Rather than return home, she moved into a small apartment on the edge of town. She managed to find a job as an administrative assistant at a law office. She told her parents that she needed a break from school and had been offered a position with opportunity for growth and advancement. She left the hallowed halls of Stanford and never looked back. She believed it was another black mark on her soul.

As time went by, Naomi became more distant from her family and friends. Initially, she returned home once a year to see her parents, enduring cold and perfunctory visits. Over time, Naomi stopped visiting them altogether. It was simply too painful and too futile an exercise. Her phone calls to them became less frequent because she couldn't stand to hear the disappointment in their voices. She eventually stopped calling and drifted away into a life where she was cut off from anyone who knew her or expected anything from her. Their phone calls landed in her voice mail and were never returned. It was easier that way. She believed she could create a new life for herself and they could let her go.

Naomi decided to change her image to change her life. She cut her long dark hair into a short, edgy style, and began to dress more provocatively. She frequented bars and nightclubs on weekends where she'd meet various men. Most nights she would stumble home with one of them, wrapped in a foggy haze of stale cigarettes and too much vodka. She'd frequently have blackouts, finding herself in the morning in yet another stranger's bed. These episodes left her sullied with shame. Naomi would exit those scenarios as quickly as she entered them, leaving behind a little more of her self-esteem and taking away a greater belief that she was worthless.

Naomi was plagued by a deep and growing anger within her, a twisted and agonizing resentment that pulsated in her veins. The more she denied this anger, the more she careened into recklessness. Rather than one-night stands, Naomi began to have relationships with different men whom she met. It seemed that each man was the same as the next, all of them empty, crass, and harsh. With each meaningless relationship, Naomi seemed to shrink further into herself. Over time, the relationships became more demanding and frightening, each escalating in intensity from the last. What began as shouting insults soon progressed to pushing and slapping. Eventually, Naomi found that she had become a mere punching bag for various men, all of whom seemed to have a powerful hold on her. She stumbled in and out of these violent relationships, unable to determine why these men couldn't see her worth or value. She craved love and acceptance but in turn found rage and abuse.

Naomi felt further away from the person she wanted to be than ever before. She woke up one morning and looked at herself in the bathroom mirror. Her hangover from the previous night's escapade left her stomach rolling and churning. She had a black eye, a cruel parting gift from her latest "boyfriend." He had punched her in the face because she'd fallen asleep on his couch. She was also missing patches of hair from where he had dragged her upstairs before forcing sex upon her. She was home now, in her tiny and lonely apartment. She ran to the toilet and vomited. She was so tired of this life and her own self-imprisonment. Although she had always mocked the idea of Alcoholics Anonymous to friends who had spoken of it to her before, she had a fleeting thought that maybe it could help.

Later that day, and for the following months, Naomi attended regular Alcoholics Anonymous meetings. At first, she sat stonily as she heard others talk of their struggles with alcohol, with life, with their past. She didn't allow herself to find or make connections with others. She was too afraid of judgment—theirs and her own. Eventually, however, she began to recognize herself reflected in their stories. She shared her story for the first time and was met with complete acceptance and support from those around her.

Naomi's willingness to open up to others correlated with longer periods of sobriety and an increased sense of responsibility for herself. She stopped frequenting bars and nightclubs and began to form more meaningful relationships with sober coworkers and friends. She took a break from romantic relationships until she could truly learn to love and respect herself. There were many lonely nights where Naomi missed the comfort of vodka, but she was learning to enjoy her own company. At those times, she often thought of her parents and what it would be like to call them. She was plagued by guilt over how she had disappeared from their lives. But she knew that they would criticize the mistakes she had made and that she would be plagued with a sense of failure. She didn't want to be reminded that she was ungrateful or how they had suffered for her. She would call them when she was more certain of herself and her life was back on track. She wanted to do something they would be proud of—something that she could be proud of, too.

On a quiet evening at home, Naomi sat reading—a passion she had rediscovered from her younger years. The phone rang, startling her from her book. It was unusual for her to get a phone call these days. Curious, she looked at the phone display. It was an out-of-town number that she didn't recognize. She answered, feeling a growing sense of unease and a premonition that something was wrong. "Hello, may I speak with Naomi please?" said the caller. "This is Lydia. I am a social worker from St. Elizabeth's Hospital. I am calling to inform you that your parents were involved in a terrible accident. I am so sorry to tell you that they both passed away at the scene. I believe you are their only child?" Naomi was uncertain how the phone call ended with the social worker or the exact details of the call. She only knew one thing: her parents were both dead—gone in a moment.

At the funeral, Naomi stood rigid as her parents' caskets were lowered solemnly into the earth. The biting cold wind carried away the last words spoken by the rabbi as dirt was tossed on the casket, per tradition, and mourners hung their heads. Naomi was surrounded by family and friends whom she hadn't seen in many years. They held her and comforted her with a warmth that seemed foreign to her. She allowed herself to be embraced by this sense of love and caring. She was so hungry to belong and so tired of feeling so empty.

Later, Naomi and her family gathered for Shiva, the Jewish period of mourning that lasts for seven days. Naomi was surprised to feel such a peaceful connection to the family that she'd walked away from so many years ago. They fed her, allowed her to sleep, and told her stories about her parents that filled Naomi with a sense of wonder.

These were stories she had never heard before—stories about her father's accomplishments and her mother's kindnesses. Naomi found herself filled with pride and yearning to learn more about the two people who had seemed like strangers. She had only known them as her parents—two wounded people who had survived Majdanek—not as people who lived lives of purpose or meaning. Naomi had always seen them through her own eyes, through her own desperation and pain. Now she was gifted with the opportunity to see them through the eyes of others.

As evening approached, Naomi sat outside, sipping a cup of hot tea. Tears slid from her eyes, making soft splashes into her cup. Naomi felt sore and breathless, as though she had been carrying a heavy weight up a long hill. Her aunt came outside to join her, settling quietly into the chair beside her. Naomi looked up and met her eyes; her aunt smiled. "She loved you, you know," her aunt said. "Your mother loved you so very much. She was so proud of you—always bragging about you: 'Naomi this, and Naomi that.'" Her aunt chuckled. Naomi looked up, startled by what she just heard. Her mother was proud of her? She loved her? "I found this in her room," her aunt said, "I thought you might want to see it." She handed Naomi a folded letter, which Naomi took and set aside; she would read it later, when she was alone.

It was close to midnight when Naomi climbed into bed. She unfolded the letter. The handwriting was beautiful, written in her mother's elegant hand:

Naomi,

It has been a few years since I last saw you. The beauty of your face still haunts me and I miss you. You were always beautiful to me. Did you know that? I was always so afraid to celebrate your beauty for fear that you would become vain or spoiled. But you are neither of those things. In fact, I often sense that you were cherished by many. I am afraid that I have failed you in this respect.

I keep hoping that you will return home one day or that you will just reach out to us. It feels like you have run so very far away. Are you running from us or from yourself? Maybe that is an unfair question, but it feels a little like both things. I hope you find what you are searching for out there, and when you do, I hope you can find it in your heart to see me one more time.

You have always been our salvation and a reminder that our lives did not end in Majdanek. The Nazis tried so hard to take away everything from us and to rid the world of our very existence. But they failed and we survived. Our early years as your parents must have reflected such a great deal of our turmoil and for that, I am truly sorry. We realize that we are free now and nothing can take that away from us. I hope you can find a way to be free, too.

I will always wait for you with an open heart.

Love,

Mother

Naomi wept as she read the letter that night, and she continued to read it to herself over and over as the years passed. The words from her mother were a healing balm on Naomi's heart. She never realized how much her suffering mirrored the suffering of her parents. Later, she read about *ancestral trauma*—the idea that traumatic suffering can alter the genetic code of a human being and then be passed down to the next generation. Naomi became a student of her past and found such healing in understanding her family and herself. She was able to recognize that she blamed herself for her parents' pain and sorrow, and she believed she could change it for them. She felt guilty for sur-viving—for just being—and took responsibility for things that she did not cause and could not change. It was only when she began to take responsibility for herself that she could be free from her self-impris-onment and live a life of integrity and honesty. This was the essence of her recovery. She sensed that her parents would have been proud of the person she had become, and of whom she would be in the future.

In 1999, Naomi made an epic journey, a rite of passage for one who bore the generational scars of evil and hatred. She walked sol-emnly and bravely through the grounds of Majdanek State Museum in Poland. She listened to her heart pounding in her ears, the bile of sadness and anger burning in her heart. It is the same painful wound that chiseled her courage to be there—to bear witness for her parents and for herself. She wept as she honored those in her family and of her faith who did not survive. She acknowledged their existence, their spirits, and their hearts. She stood before the mausoleum, containing ashes of those who died there. A cool breeze lifted strands of her hair but the sun warmed her back, and gave her a sense of resolute peace. Transfixed, she stood there, remembering the stories, the fear, and the pain that had defined her life for so long. Then, she willed herself to let go, to free herself of the darkness. She reached in the pocket of her jacket for the small polished stone, and finding it, stroked it with her fingers one last time. She turned the stone over and read the words that she had etched into it: I am free, I am strong. She bent down and left the stone near a tree. She walked away, back to the car and her life, with all its wonderful possibilities.

～

SIX

GRATITUDE

THE WORDS "THANK YOU" ARE THE MOST DIRECT route to the destination of appreciation and connection. Notice how you feel the next time you hear or say them. Typically you'll feel a charge of positive energy and a quick dose of warmth. Research indicates that the expression of gratitude on a regular basis increases positive outcomes personally and professionally. When we feel genuinely appreciated, we are more likely to find motivation to create and make things happen. Articulating appreciation for others creates feelings of well-being, generating momentum for more positive feelings, and giving us reasons to be grateful for all the good in our lives. Practicing and expressing gratitude improves relationships, generates positive outcomes, and increases feelings of joy. The opposite of trauma is freedom and joy; gratitude helps to get us there.

Gratitude cannot produce the same benefits if it is expressed because of an expectation or obligation. Many clients I work with struggle with a gratitude practice because the message was drilled in by members of their family of origin that they should be *more* grateful. Forced gratitude is strained, produces shame, and is very different than choosing to notice the good. Habitual gratitude can be helpful, but only if we are mindful of it. For instance, we are supposed to be grateful during holidays, such as Thanksgiving, but this might be more of an automatic response than one that is genuine. To really receive the optimal, beneficial results of gratitude we need to be awake and alive to fully absorb the feeling. Stumbling around in a tryptophan-induced malaise after the Thanksgiving Day feast, grateful to score a deal during Black Friday once a year, doesn't quite meet the requirements for an actual gratitude practice. There is a horn of plenty filled with abundance, always available for us, if we develop a vision to see it and the willingness to celebrate it. A daily practice of gratitude directly relates to finding the essence of resilience. When we are looking for the gifts in our lives, we are more likely to see them and treasure them, and anticipate more offerings of goodness in the future.

The research to support gratitude practice is irrefutable and abundant. Numerous studies indicate that verbalizing or writing just a few gratitude statements helps to regulate mood, and reduces stress and potential for relapse with addictions while promoting feelings of contentment. Gratitude practice is commonly used as a resource in twelve-step programs when individuals fighting for their recovery start slipping and succumbing to their resentments, triggers, and addictive cravings. Gratitude grounds us and creates an emotional safety zone. Focusing on gratitude changes our energy by shifting our perspective; rather than feeling depleted, we feel inspired. As a trauma therapist I experience gratitude firsthand on a regular basis while working with clients and sharing in their experiences. What a privilege it is to be invited into a client's world, to understand their story, and journey with them through their emotional and cognitive landscapes! I am in awe of the many brave clients that I've had the opportunity to observe and join as they come through their dark tunnels of suffering to find their internal light. I can't imagine a more rewarding task. Frequently, I hear secrets that have festered for years, that have occupied visceral space in the minds, hearts, and bodies of my clients. Often, trauma survivors transcending the weight and depth of their suffering experience gratitude for their growing strength and resilience. Sharing stories of trauma can be heartbreaking and overwhelming, but they also illuminate the resilience of the human spirit.

Many trauma survivors, especially if the trauma occurred during childhood, internalize their suffering and feel shameful and responsible for it. Sometimes the psychological and physiological symptoms of post-traumatic stress linger long after the trauma occurred. The past trauma often plays in a repetitive loop in their minds and continues to hold the survivor hostage to current experiences of fear and stress. This is when a gratitude practice can help survivors find their resilience.

Even the act of taking a breath can be painful for trauma survivors, who can find themselves overwhelmed with anxiety and heartbreak, manifesting as a heavy weight on their chests. Breathing again fully can be the very place to begin practicing gratitude. While cultivating a feeling of gratitude for a tragic loss, a life-threatening experience, or the violation of integrity is unrealistic, the survivor who made it through to this present moment, who is still breathing, can focus on the breath, living in the present moment, and being grateful for the experience.

Part of the healing process is the often-recommended and necessary step of letting go: letting go of the past, letting go of a person, letting go of old beliefs and memories. While valuable, this action may seem unattainable for trauma survivors who are riddled with symptoms of fear, flashbacks, and triggers that unexpectedly bring them back to their painful past. The wound of trauma can become like a black hole, sucking energy into a dark pit. To begin finding resolution and healing is the ability to not only let go of some things but also to hold on. Holding on is the practice of gratitude. It can be the difference between getting lost in the swirl of suffering, or finding a grip and grabbing on to life again. All of our senses provide us with opportunities for gratitude: watching a vibrant sunrise, looking into a loved one's eyes, noticing the details on a flower petal, hearing the sound of a heartbeat, feeling the brush of a dog's cold wet nose, listening to beautiful music, or experiencing the warmth of connection.

With gratitude we can choose to focus on our gifts instead of our losses. In every chapter of our lives there is a nugget or treasure for which we can be grateful. We can remember the past in a safe and soothing way, we can embrace the present, and we can imagine a bright future. As part of a gratitude practice we can venture inside of ourselves and appreciate qualities that have been there all along, like caring, creativity, passion, or determination. We truly have an endless resource of healing within the practice of gratitude.

This chapter's story is about a trauma survivor, Eliza, who lost support and stability as a very young child. Being grateful and literally holding on to something she cherished helped her to survive. Eliza's creativity and willingness to express herself transformed her pain into something meaningful and beautiful. In the story, she demonstrates tremendous courage and strength through gratitude, and in the process finds her voice and creates a life filled with music, abundance, and love.

"When I started counting my blessings
my whole life turned around."

—*Willie Nelson*

Eliza: A Song of Love and Gratitude

Her grandma's apron was the safest place she knew. She kept it after her grandmother died and would hold it when she felt scared, remembering her grandmother's smell, her spirit, and how nurtured she felt with her. Even as an adult she wrapped herself in the soft cotton of the apron like a blanket. Eliza was intelligent and understood the need for children to attach to something. As a girl, the only time she felt secure and attached to someone was during the fleeting summers she spent with her grandmother. Now that she was gone, the piece of cloth was the closest thing to a relational attachment she had. At times, it seemed the apron came alive for Eliza. The childlike part of her believed that it gave her special powers and would help guide her to overcome her struggles. With the torment and suffering she'd endured throughout her life, she needed a little magic and support. Not a day passed when Eliza wasn't grateful for the loving influence of her grandmother, and for the warmth and security she felt while holding her apron.

By the time she was eighteen, Eliza had moved twenty times, through many towns—never calling any one place home. From Eliza's early childhood until she became an adult she was dragged around like a limp doll, following the chaotic cycles of her father's instability. He was an angry alcoholic who had difficulty maintaining relationships, especially with his employers. He lacked insight and was incapable of taking responsibility for his actions. Eliza's mother had been the love of his life, and when she died he was filled with anger, overcome with feelings of bitterness, and believed the world was full of the ethos of injustice. Eliza's father's rage was ever present, no matter where they moved. Eliza often hid and tried to stay out of his way, bracing herself for the next outburst. She felt like her existence was a burden, and her presence in her father's life only triggered him, reminding him of her mother and all that had been stripped from his life. She could almost anticipate when the wrath would come. As the empty beer cans piled up and the volume of his voice grew, piercing the air, she knew blows would follow. He would unleash his fury, breaking things and yelling, and then he'd go after Eliza. Lying crumpled on the floor, her face covered with bruises, she felt trapped with her father, powerless and bound together in their brokenness. Afterward he would leave, slamming the door behind him—sometimes for days.

Eventually, Eliza would pick herself up and make it back to her room where she would find her grandmother's apron and hold it as she hid in her closet. She would cry and curl up into a ball, hugging her knees, rocking back and forth, and wishing her life were different. As the apron absorbed her tears, she'd envision herself leaving, drifting away to another existence. After a while she would start humming, remembering the sound of her grandmother's voice, and how the two of them would harmonize . Then Eliza would begin to sing. She'd create her own sound: words turned into lyrics, developed with rhythms that made sense to her in the midst of a reality that made no sense. Soon she created her own playlist of different songs about her pain, about her mother dying when she was two years old, about the rage of her father and how much he was hurting her. Her voice erupted from the darkness as an expression of her truest self. Eliza released an energy that allowed her to travel anywhere in her closet. She could soar on the jet streams of her voice, and transcend the pain of her current circumstances. Through the ache and sadness she began to feel free. She didn't fear her father now, he wouldn't be coming home for a while and he never hurt her in her closet when she was singing.

Eliza wondered what her life would be like if her mother didn't get cancer and die when she was two. She tried to imagine her mother's face, her eyes, and the sound of her voice. People would tell Eliza that her face was a virtual replica of her mother's. They'd say that her mother, like her maternal grandmother, had a beautiful voice. Holding on to her grandmother's apron and singing was the only way she knew to hold on to her family heritage, her legacy, and possibly access some of her mother's energy. Sometimes when she sang she felt the flow of connection moving through her like a familiar, generational energy, connecting Eliza with her grandmother—her mother—through her voice. She craved the feeling of being nurtured and wished she could have felt the sensation of her mother brushing her hair, telling her stories, or singing her lullabies. She had a hard time envisioning a nuclear family and a functioning father. She knew that her father was always an alcoholic and had problems controlling his anger, but when her mother died, she'd been told, something broke inside him, unleashing a force of extreme rage and addiction. Eliza only experienced the fragmented remnants of her father and she wondered what he'd been like before. Was he handsome, generous, and maybe even tender at times? She knew he was capable of loving because he loved her mother so much. Eliza would often find him passed out on the couch, clutching her mother's picture in his hand. The sad truth of the matter was that, even though her father was alive, Eliza had no parents. Her father was dead, spiritually and emotionally. She was an emotional orphan, and the loneliness that went along with that was at times unbearable.

Before her grandmother died when Eliza was eight, she would spend the summers with her. Every year she wished the summers would last forever. As soon as she stepped out of her father's truck in her grandmother's driveway she felt a breeze of relief. Her grandmother would greet her with a big smile, dressed in her apron (whether she was cooking or not), and wrap Eliza in her arms. The house was white and charming, surrounded by fields of grass. As Eliza grew, she would envision this house as a safe place—the only place she could recall that felt like home. It was often filled with music, and Eliza and her grandma would hum along together, harmonizing and singing. Eliza could play and be herself, feeling comfortable with her grandma in a way that she felt with no one else.

Much like the blossoming flowers in the garden, her grandmother's nurturing and kindness helped Eliza's true personality emerge. Feeling free and loved, she spontaneously opened to the natural rhythms of life. Though she wanted to pretend as if her life with her father didn't exist, it would creep up on her, especially at night, and memories would come back, reminding her of the fear and anticipation of the abuse. Sometimes, in the midst of a peaceful moment with her grandma, a surge of emotion would surface, and Eliza would instantly start sobbing uncontrollably. When her grandmother asked her why she was crying, she'd just answer, "I don't know. I just feel sad for no reason." She never told her grandmother or anyone about the beatings; even in the safety of her grandmother's arms she couldn't say the words. The memories would flood through her, sometimes because of a trigger like the smell of beer, or a sound similar to the snap of a belt, which made her think of her father's drunken rage. Other times it was the safety of the connection with her grandmother that would elicit an outpouring of emotions—with her she was safe to release them, unlike with her father. Somehow it wasn't so awful, or so real, if she kept this inside and didn't speak of it—even with her grandmother. Eliza knew it wasn't her fault but she also felt that she was responsible for participating in the abuse, and felt scared and embarrassed that this was her story and part of her identity. Even if her grandmother didn't know the reason for her tears, Eliza still felt very loved and supported. Her grandmother's apron, which held her calm and loving energy, was like a nest that Eliza could curl up into. During those summers, a part of Eliza began to believe that her life was precious, and she deserved to be loved at least by one person.

One day, Eliza's father informed her that her grandmother died of a heart attack. He just blurted it out, like the weather report, his delivery cold and unfeeling, and Eliza mirrored him, displaying a numb effect herself. She had been grieving for so long that she felt tapped out, as though she had no more tears or sadness left. She knew that summers would never be the same but she held on to the feeling of warmth inside her heart. The memory of their connection defended her on the inside from the brutality and chaos of life with her father. Thankfully, Eliza inherited the apron—the most precious item she could imagine from her grandmother's house. She held onto it like she was still holding on to her grandma, filled with gratitude. She kept the apron hidden in her closet and felt cheerful when she could see the lace trim or faded pink gingham peeking out from behind her other clothes. It became her solace and her lifeline.

As Eliza grew into adolescence, her father kept drinking, drowning in liquor and despair. Tired and listless, it seemed he no longer had the strength to break objects or hurt Eliza. Instead, he would sink into his usual spot on the sagging sofa and pass out. Eliza would sometimes stare at his snoring face, watching him sucking for air to inhale and rattling out a loud exhale. She never understood how he could hit her, and wondered if he was trying to break everything around him because he felt so broken inside. As much as he had hurt her, it pained Eliza to watch her father's destructive downward spiral. She wished she could help him, and tried to support him the best she could, but she realized she couldn't mend him, and he didn't want her help or recovery for himself. Sometimes when she sang in her closet she hoped that he could hear her, and that her voice would soften his hurt and his anger, but he never seemed to notice or care. He was deaf to her voice and blind to her suffering. His own complicated grief—in which he'd lost himself and his connection with his daughter—drowned out the space between them. In her heart, Eliza knew that if she didn't leave eventually, she would get pulled down with him. The only place where there was air for her to breathe was within the confines of her closet.

That's where Eliza found herself and her voice. She spent so much time there crying and singing, the closet became her world where she could explore and play by singing different styles and experimenting with different methods. She challenged herself to constantly change her sound, molding it and reshaping it again. She channeled all of her distress into her passion. She sang jazz, country, and folk; she even tried singing in different languages. She imagined performing in front of audiences and could feel her grandmother cheering her on. Even though she was alone she began to grow in confidence in herself, and in her voice. She felt a growing urge to open the door, step into her life, and connect to others through music.

Although Eliza wanted friends, shame about her circumstances made her hesitant to socialize. She became adept at ducking out of social situations, allowing her to keep a safe distance. Whenever she did start to warm up to other people and trust enough to entertain the thought of a friendship, she and her father were off to a new town, forced to uproot and start over again. This exhausting pattern wore

Eliza down making it virtually impossible to maintain any kind of friendship, let alone a lasting one.

Part of her appreciated the transient lifestyle. She lived in many cities across the southeast. The diversity quenched her curiosity and offered the opportunity to observe new places and cultures. She applied the variety of experiences to expand the range and complexity of her voice. Still, she felt profoundly lonely, and she desperately craved attachment to someone besides her emotionally unavailable father. She wanted to connect with a community and feel a part of something meaningful. She hoped that her music could become the bridge that allowed her to cross over the river of isolation to connect with others.

Just before Eliza turned eighteen, they moved to yet another new place—she hoped for the last time. At her new high school she took a chance and joined the musical theater group. The thought of singing in front of her peers and teachers was terrifying at first, but the anxiety disappeared the minute she opened her mouth to sing. Eliza was appreciated for her talents and was selected for lead parts in shows and musicals. She allowed herself to be vulnerable and be seen for the first time. Simultaneously, she feared that history would repeat itself and that she'd get the rug pulled out from under her with another move just as she was beginning to blossom and grow. She decided that this time she couldn't move; this was the first time—outside of her closet—that she felt settled and safe.

Eliza joined a band with some of her theater friends, and they started to play gigs around town. Eliza kept her tips and earnings folded up in her grandmother's apron in her closet. She was surprised at how much she had collected in just a few months. Eliza began searching for someplace to live with her music friends. Through her search for independence, she realized that there were many options, and after feeling helpless for so long, finally knew she had the ability to become self-reliant and resourceful.

With her eighteenth birthday just a few weeks away, she'd saved enough to cover basic living expenses for six months. At the same time, her father was exhibiting the signs he usually did before a move—complaining about his job and searching for new work in other areas, cursing his employer, and drinking more. Like clockwork, he told her that they would be moving to a new city next month. Eliza wanted to tell him how much she loved where they lived now, but she knew that would start a fight and force her to justify her choices, neither of which she wanted. She just needed to hang on until she was legally able to make her own move. The morning after she turned eighteen she woke up before dawn. With her bags packed in her arms, she tiptoed out through the living room to where her father lay passed out on the sofa, snoring like a freight train. She bent over and kissed him on the forehead, whispering, "Good-bye, Dad." He didn't stir. Eliza left the room, no longer tiptoeing, and walked out into the dark, cold morning.

Eliza became known throughout the local music community, and she performed frequently as a solo artist and with different bands. She was developing a reputation nationally for her unique and soulful sound. She connected with the audience in such a profoundly emotional way that people often left her shows in tears. The response and appreciation for her music shocked Eliza but it also felt natural, an affirmation that she was meant to sing. Even when performing in front of hundreds of people, she still felt like that girl alone in her closet, unconscious of her surroundings, connecting with the truth of her pain, coming from her core.

Before long she signed with a record label and sales of her album accelerated. In time, Eliza received an abundance of rewards and financial security that she had never known before. People were singing along with her lyrics in cars and living rooms all over the country. Her fame and fortune rose beyond anything she could have anticipated. While she appreciated the glamour and attention that she received, what she cherished most were the moments when she felt the emotional and soulful connection with her audience. As she shared her grief and her heart, Eliza felt the audience tuning in to the emotion, sharing a heart connection through her music.

The introverted part of Eliza still appreciated time alone away from the bright stage lights. She cherished mornings where she could sit and relax with a cup of coffee gazing out the window of the house she bought herself, enjoying the river view. At these times she would reflect with gratitude about all of the abundance in her life. Sitting and watching the river became a ritual and gave Eliza a feeling of peace. Every morning she would walk by her kitchen pantry where her grandmother's apron was hanging, would take a moment to hold the fabric, and whisper, *Thank you.*

Eliza was proud of her accomplishments; still, there was a vacancy inside of her, reminiscent of the loneliness and pain of the past. She had hoped that time, achievement, and success would fill this hollowness, but the feeling never left.

Eliza felt content in her lifestyle and with her own company but she also wanted to open herself up to more intimate relationships, and find a loving connection in her present circumstances. In the context of singing she felt safe with vulnerability within the structure of her music, but offstage she felt scared. Emotional intimacy terrified her. She knew she could go on like this on her own, and no one would ever know about her past. It would remain her secret. But Eliza wanted more. She wanted to heal the grief, and feel free from the past. She wanted to find connection and love that didn't require a performance.

Eliza decided to use her voice differently for the first time, and tell the whole truth about her childhood. She began therapy and at first felt terrified and awkward. But soon the floodgates began to open. She said the words that were implied in her music, but had never been explicitly articulated. She spoke about the loss of her mother, and the chasm that was left in her heart and in her view of the world around her. For the first time she spoke about the abuse she had suffered with her father, how he hit her, and how much he broke her. While Eliza sobbed, grief poured out of her, in a rush of physical sensations. What she experienced felt like transcendence, washing away grief and leaving an opening to welcome in new beginnings.

Eliza had experienced many romantic interludes but never allowed herself to truly unfold with another person. Her fear was, if he saw how damaged she was, her pursuer would turn around and run in the opposite direction. She often didn't trust the motives of those interested in her, and hypothesized that sharing in the shine of her celebrity status was their primary attraction. At the same time, she had many relationships that were genuinely caring. One of her motivations for beginning therapy was due to the budding relationship with a friend that was moving into romantic domain. He was gentle and kind, secure in his musical talent and respected Eliza. She felt like he could see her pain and feel it through her music, but he wasn't intimidated, instead he was curious. They had been dating for months and Eliza, despite all the barriers she had built up against it, found she was succumbing to feelings of love.

While in therapy Eliza became more open to a committed relationship and took the leap to open up more fully. She focused on working hard to shed her grief and abuse from the past because she didn't want to carry resentments or bitterness into this precious beginning of opening herself up to love. In therapy she worked on understanding the story of her past, remembering how much she loved singing in her closet. Her therapist asked her what she found alone in her closet, holding her grandmother's apron and singing. Through tears, Eliza said, "My voice."

Eliza felt incredible gratitude for her voice and understood how many gifts came to her through her natural instrument. Everything beautiful in her life had come to her through music, and through the sound she found coming through her in the depths of her trauma. Through her voice she found creativity, spirituality, a career, security, and love.

With her therapist, Eliza visualized herself as a child in the closet, bruised, alone, crying, and singing. She imagined going to her, opening the door, and leading her out of the closet, dancing and singing with her like her grandmother used to do. By opening the closet door, she opened her heart and was able to sing and dance her way into love and intimacy.

~

SEVEN

GRIT

AS A TRAUMA THERAPIST I'VE HAD THE OPPORTUNITY to work with some of the bravest, strongest, most tenacious individuals that I can imagine. Not only have they survived horrendous traumas, they are also willing to come regularly to therapy and do the necessary and often painful work; to grow and transform through their losses, becoming more open, more present, and more vulnerable in their recovery. It requires grit—determination and courage—to pull yourself up and get through the nights and days after a traumatic blow. The German philosopher Friedrich Nietzsche said, "That which doesn't kill us, makes us stronger." Following this adage, trauma survivors, who have endured so much hardship and suffering, are powerful indeed.

Sometimes grit and abrasive substances, like people, can be difficult to deal with. Individuals with this characteristic can sometimes come across as stubborn, manipulative, argumentative, high maintenance, and unnecessarily competitive. Especially in adolescence, behaviors that could promote grit and determination seem troublesome and oppositional. This feistiness or tenacity can be the very thing that helps an individual survive. That spirit that refuses to give up, even while surviving painful and overwhelming circumstances, is the resilience of the human spirit. Grit provides traction to stay grounded when the world and emotional responses are spinning out of control from the chaos that results from trauma.

Persistence is one of the most important parts of healing trauma and accessing resilience. The impact of trauma can emotionally knock a person to the ground in shock and pain. It's understandable, maybe even natural, and certainly easy to want to stay down and surrender to the loss and the pain.

Some of the most resilient people are not necessarily the most intelligent, or the most talented, highly skilled, or gifted, but they are the ones who keep fighting. Even when they are down, they find the energy and a reason to keep working, and they actualize their dreams. Grit helps identify the reason and put it into action. Many trauma survivors have had to develop tenacity out of necessity just to keep breathing. Trauma survivors can utilize the stress response of hyperarousal, and the fight to survive to regain meaning in their lives. When all the energy and adrenaline that is released and charged through trauma can be channeled to fight for recovery, for meaning, for purpose, or for a legacy, then resilience and triumph can be found.

The next story is about Maynard. The youngest of two boys, he's feisty, loves his family, and cherishes their time and connection together until his world is turned upside down. Maynard survives and witnesses a horrendous loss that haunts him in such a profound way that at first, his only recourse is to turn to addiction. As Maynard begins to make peace with and accept the loss, he realizes he needs to fight for his own survival, and in doing so, learns to honor and then find himself again. Maynard never gives up. With grit and determination he discovers his own resilience while honoring the legacy of his family.

"Never, never, never give up."

—*Winston Churchill*

Maynard: The Grit to Wrestle
Free of His Pain

Maynard was the youngest in his family. When he and his brother, John, who was three years his senior, sometimes even his father would pile up and wrestle on the living room floor. Maynard would usually end up on the bottom. He would struggle under his brother's and father's weight while they all shook with laughter. When Maynard could no longer tolerate the odors coming off them, or the humiliation, he would find the strength and determination to overpower his brother and father and wrestle out of the position. In spite of his age, he could nevertheless compete with his older brother and his friends in any kind of physical or intellectual challenge. Maynard had a reputation for his relentless spirit, never giving up even when others would likely throw in the towel in the same situation.

Growing up, Maynard, John, and their father spent fall weekends watching football on television, each donning their favorite player's jersey. Commenting on the game, trash-talking, and cracking jokes until they would all fall over, cramping from laughter, was the usual course of events. Sometimes a dispute could not be resolved verbally by sitting on the couch, so it would escalate and turn into a physical throw down on the shag carpet. Maynard's mother would witness the raucous energy and smile with pride until she'd step in to referee. Instead of blowing a whistle, she'd bring plates of snacks—the best diversion to restore civility—then the entire family would recline on the sofa enjoying snacks, the game, and each other.

The memories of those moments in the family living room filled Maynard with warmth and joy. He loved his family with all of his heart. He didn't mind the wrestling, and felt like he earned respect from his father and brother because he would always find a way to beat them, even though he was much smaller. Sometimes during the games, John would pat him on the shoulder or his father would scratch his head with affection. When Maynard's friends and his brother's friends came over to their house, they would often comment on how much they wished their families were more like Maynard's. His home exuded warmth, love, camaraderie, and playfulness. Maynard understood how special his family was, and he felt grateful. Maynard could move with confidence in his activities, orbiting back around to his family system, which provided him with safety and organization. He felt the balance between them, and the support—like a gravitational pull that would always bring him home.

Outside his house, Maynard approached everything with the same tenacity that he used when he wrestled on the living room floor. He didn't fear coming from behind, and he embraced the perception of being the underdog because he knew his grit and perseverance would help him overcome any challenge in the end. As the youngest, he was consistently at a disadvantage competing with his big brother and often with his brother's friends who were his senior. In addition, when it came to debates or disputes, Maynard's sharp and swift wit, coupled with his eloquence, ensured that he would cut through the core of the argument and would have the final word.

While Maynard excelled in most everything he did, John had a more difficult time, stumbling and struggling with academics and athletics. As his brother grew older, entering middle school, he became discouraged, depressed, and confused about who he was and what he might become. It appeared to Maynard that his brother's priorities had shifted, his values departing from those of his family's. Their strong bond began to fracture. Although there was no unusual discourse or conflict, John started drifting and changing course; the "gravity" that once pulled him back toward Maynard and his family was losing its force.

Maynard's brother began spending more time away from the house, and when he got to high school, even spending the night with new acquaintances. Maynard later learned that John was using cannabis and prescription drugs that Maynard had never heard of. The family jersey-wearing football-watching ritual occurred less regularly, and without the same energy or enthusiasm. Instead, John created rituals with his new friends, who weren't acquainted with the family, usually involving drug use. Maynard knew that John couldn't stick around and be his best friend forever, but this change in their relationship was abrupt and very distressing.

Maynard was determined not to let his brother drift away completely, so he began asking his brother if he could come with him to meet his friends. When his brother said that was okay, Maynard felt elated to finally have the opportunity to bond again with his brother. Maynard was nervous about the drug use that would likely take place, but when the bong was passed to him Maynard didn't hesitate to partake. He missed bonding with his brother, and, as he choked on the smoke, he hoped this would help win back his brother. Before long, the outings became habitual. Maynard wasn't always invited but when his brother said, "You can come," as he nodded at him to jump into his pickup truck, he eagerly complied. His eagerness was not because he wanted to do drugs, and he certainly didn't care for his brother's new friends; it was all about wanting to reestablish the bond with his brother. Maynard didn't see the danger in his own drug use, which he considered experimentation.

Maynard noticed that his brother often seemed lost and depressed, which worried him, but when he was intoxicated he would laugh and joke, like he used to before in their living room. Seeing him happy was a relief, even if it was chemically induced. Still, deep down, Maynard worried about him. He had a fear that his brother would keep circling down the more he used, and the more he used, the more depressed and lost he seemed. Maynard felt like he was chasing his brother, using drugs as a way—the only way—to catch him. As they'd grown older, the only thing they seemed to have in common was sports. It certainly wasn't school. His brother couldn't understand why Maynard was so focused on academics and why he was planning for college. His brother showed no desire to go to college and was drifting aimlessly, without focus, or any future aspirations.

This all seemed to change one evening when Maynard's brother joined him out on the family basketball court, where they sat down and had a heart-to-heart talk. Maynards brother apologized for introducing him to drugs, and spoke about how he needed to change his life, which would include moving away to join the army. Maynard was glad that his brother, on his own, realized that his drug use was a problem, and was willing to take action to change, and find recovery. Maynard knew that his brother was trying to become a better mentor to him, but he couldn't hold back the tears, which he wiped away on the sleeve of his T-shirt as he nodded with understanding. He was relieved about his brother's decision to get clean, but he had a feeling of dread about what could happen to him in the army. He would miss John, of course, and he hoped that his unsettled feelings were just because of that.

Maynard's brother enlisted and was gone for three years. During that time he was deployed to Iraq. His brother kept in contact and they had some good family connections through FaceTime, e-mails, letters, and phone calls. From all of the reports, Maynard's brother was thriving in the army, and the more Maynard heard from him, the less lonely his brother seemed, so Maynard's worry subsided. Maynard admired his brother for finding an honorable purpose, and respected his choice to serve his country. Geographically, they were very far from each other, but Maynard felt like they were moving in the same orbit again and the balance of forces was back. His brother had changed his life and now was living in accordance with the family values. His identity was shaping into one of service, honor, and integrity. Maynard's admiration and respect for his brother grew. Maynard stopped using any drugs and had no desire to anymore. Inspired by his brother, Maynard excelled in his own achievements and felt a renewed ease and confidence.

Maynard was preparing to graduate from high school when his brother finally came home on leave. The family organized a celebratory homecoming to welcome him back and honor his service. When Maynard met his brother at the airport it was like he was meeting a completely different person. He seemed stiff, almost frozen. He moved slowly, dragging his feet and staring at the ground to avoid eye contact with anyone. Occasionally, his brother would look up like he saw something that wasn't there, his eyes staring off into the distance, like he was searching for something.

At home, his brother went through the motions of celebrating, but he seemed hollow. That night, and every night, his brother woke up yelling and screaming from terrible nightmares. He told his family that he had post-traumatic stress disorder from combat, and that the symptoms would go away in time. The family understood the reasons for the symptoms, but they all felt worried and helpless, especially Maynard.

Through all of this, Maynard worked hard to stay focused on his finals, and successfully earned his high school diploma, graduating with honors. During his graduation ceremony, however, he noticed that his brother wasn't there. It was strange because his brother promised he'd be there. Afterward they all were supposed to go out to their favorite restaurant.

After the ceremony Maynard and his family rushed home. They were understandably anxious but tried not to be alarmist. This was the day to celebrate Maynard's achievements, and his parents understood the importance of that. Still, as they all tried their best to stay calm, Maynard had this horrible feeling hammering through his stomach. He hoped he was just paranoid instead of clairvoyant. When they arrived home his brother wasn't there but his cell phone was left on his bed. Panic struck Maynard; his brother never went anywhere without his phone. His parents tried to hide their worry and informed Maynard that they would call friends, contacts, family, and the restaurant to see if he was with them. Maynard knew they were trying to remain calm but their darting eyes and trembling hands told a different story. Maynard told them that he needed to get some air and went for a walk outside.

Maynard ran out toward the woods behind the basketball court. Behind their property the woods stretched for miles. Maynard and his brother used to explore there when they were much younger and Maynard knew the way through the pines, it was their "beat." He ran for what seemed like an eternity. He didn't know what he was running from or toward but he kept moving, chasing an answer that could put his fears to rest. Out of breath, his heart pounding, he dropped to the ground, his knees and hands falling on pine needles. When he looked up through a clearing in the woods he saw a vision that was so horrible he couldn't believe it was real. From one of the branches on the trees in front of him, his brother was hanging, colorless and lifeless.

A part of Maynard died that day in the woods. His parents tried to console him, but they were so grief-stricken they were not capable of offering any meaningful support. There was no note or clear explanation for why, but everyone knew how much Maynard's brother was altered by war and how much he was suffering.

The impact of this event blew apart the once-organized orbit of their family system. The trauma and the unimaginable grief overwhelmed them as they struggled to survive. Rather than come together for solace and support, each dealt with their grief independently, moving in different but equally unhealthy ways. Maynard's mother sank into a depression. She spent hours in her bed, going for days without getting dressed or showering. Family meals were a thing of the past, and she stopped calling her friends or going outside unless she absolutely had to. His father was often gone, out at the local bar, drinking constantly. Maynard couldn't bear being in the house with all the memories, and he decided to connect with John's old friends as a way to feel closer to him. Maynard fell back into the pattern of drug use with them. This time, the experience of using was significantly more potent, and for Maynard, felt almost spiritual.

Nightmares and flashbacks of that horrible day in the woods haunted Maynard, traveling through his mind like a film clip on a perpetual loop. He was now also using chemicals to try to numb the memory of his loss. And it worked to some degree; the memories that haunted him faded away. Instead, he remembered using drugs with his brother, laughing with him when he was alive. For a few fleeting moments, under the influence, he felt bonded again with his brother. Maynard couldn't believe his brother was permanently gone, and when he was using he could forget for a while; the gaping hole in his heart would become temporarily—and artificially—filled. Every reach for the bong or the pill bottle was a desperate, futile reach for his big brother. In an intoxicated, emotion-numbing haze, he entered a state of consciousness that was bearable, and which would allow him to deny the reality about his loss. There was a price to pay for this as the frequent use soon turned into an addiction. Maynard dropped his plans to go to college and law school. Getting and using drugs became his occupation.

Members of the community, family, and friends came by bringing meals and offering condolences. Maynard appreciated these gestures but his drug use wouldn't allow him to be fully present to receive their emotional support. He greeted his guests with bloodshot eyes, and created distance between himself and most social interactions. Some assumed that he was in an altered state, but it was difficult to decipher what was happening with Maynard. Was he grieving or under the influence? For the few who assumed that he might be using drugs, there was a level of understanding, and implicit condoning and acceptance. Still, everyone missed the joyful and exuberant energy that used to reside in the house. Maynard became a phantom of the person he used to be; all the feistiness and heart seemed to have died with his brother.

Maynard's tolerance grew when it came to using pills. He had to travel now to get more of a supply, and was mixing with a criminal element. His life was threatened when he had a gun pointed at him during the transactions. Maynard still had inside him a raw determination and the fierceness to fight back, to never give up. In these situations, he used it to find ways to maneuver out of any threat.

Ironically, home was where he faced the biggest threat. Instead of physical danger he was overwhelmed by emotional blackness and an unrelenting sadness from which there was no escape. As he watched his parents, he struggled with the choices he was making that threatened his life. While Maynard was careless about his own life, having seemingly no fear when it came to drug dealers, he knew his parents could not bear to lose their only surviving son.

Knowing this, Maynard realized that he would have to fight for his life now—if not for himself, then for his parents—and would have to move through the pain and trauma of losing his brother. The heaviness of the grief and trauma was like no pileup he had ever experienced. He could wrestle himself out of almost any situation but this one he couldn't get out of alone. He recognized that he was compromised under the influence, and the strength and spirit he once had was fading, leaving him weak and susceptible. He wanted his energy and vitality back and knew he'd have to fight. He would take on his addiction the way he used to take on his opponents: with grit and determination to overcome.

After his brother died, Maynard never ventured to the backyard basketball court, or certainly beyond to the woods, because there were too many horrific and painful memories. When he made the decision to get sober he knew he would have to face the grief and the darkness, and the memories that haunted him.

One day he decided to move toward his fears. He walked out beyond the backyard into the woods, retracing his steps to the tree where he found his brother. There, he fell down to his knees and spoke to his brother as if he was still there. Maynard shook while crying out for his brother, telling him how much he missed him and how he wished he could have done something. Maynard made a commitment to get the support that his brother never had the opportunity to receive. Maynard promised John that he would remain sober for both of them, and somehow he would make his brother proud again. The verbal contract he had just made with his brother was more binding than any promise or signed document. He left the woods, this time with purpose and resilience to reclaim his life and honor his brother.

Maynard was ready to take the necessary steps to begin his recovery. He attended twelve-step meetings and identified a sponsor through Alcoholics Anonymous. He contacted a respected trauma therapist in his community. He read everything he could about PTSD, and knew he needed to focus on his grief from the horrible and devastating loss of his brother from suicide. Maynard also realized how much his brother's post-traumatic stress disorder impacted the whole family, and he wanted to learn more about why he struggled, and how he could have been helped. Maynard knew that he was also experiencing trauma symptoms, and wanted some coping strategies to learn how to handle them in a sober way. Maynard carried the remnants of that stressful day in his body and in his heart. His goal was to understand himself and his brother, and to find a pathway through all of this loss and pain to a place where he could be sober and find peace.

Maynard loved a challenge, and he embraced his recovery. He found himself initiating discussions, and was open to taking the microphone and speaking during many of the meetings. He became very close with his sponsor, and they developed a relationship that was much like that of a mentor or older brother/younger brother. He had an outlet for questions he would have asked his older brother. While he knew that the answers would never be the same as what his brother might have given him, he was grateful and open to his sponsor's individuality, and his considerable knowledge about recovery.

His sponsor didn't lose his brother like Maynard did, but he understood pain, grief, and how to maintain recovery even under stress. In the fellowship, Maynard found connection, safety, and a bond in sobriety that helped him build back his own life.

In therapy, Maynard shared stories about his brother; not only retracing the steps of that horrible day when he found him in the woods, but also recalling the loving bond that they had—the good times. Through telling the stories, Maynard felt like his brother's energy and spirit moved closer and were back within his grasp. He learned more about the neurobiological and physiological effects of trauma and had compassion for how deeply his brother must have been suffering. Maynard now understood that if he hadn't reached out and asked for help, the experience of finding his brother could have haunted him his entire life. He learned that even the most powerful and toughest person could not face trauma and addiction alone. As he progressed through recovery, he imagined that he was bringing John along with him, guiding him through the healing that could have been possible. He wished so badly that his brother had had the support to wrestle his terrors, take them down, and reduce his own pain. Since this wasn't possible, Maynard experienced recovery for him, with him. He felt his brother's support and presence through every step of the process.

Maynard returned to college, graduated, and continued on to attend and then finish law school. He was determined to create change to support recovery in the legal system. The drive to create stability and justice in his own life fueled him to transcend his own story and support justice for others. He was conscious that his need to help people was an effort to vicariously save his brother. Maynard worked diligently in therapy and in his recovery program, and understood that he didn't need to carry guilt or shame for his inability to prevent his brother's suicide. Still, Maynard felt that if he could help others receive treatment or find recovery, this would mean that his brother's death was not in vain, that his legacy would be to help others find peace. Maynard learned that his brother, and so many others who commit, suicide, are suffering deeply and carrying pain that is overwhelming. No one from the outside can imagine another person's internal anguish. Maynard always looked up to his brother and viewed him as a guide, a hero, and the life of the party. Still, his brother felt like he had no other options, and now Maynard understood why many others succumb to the same sense of hopelessness. Maynard's compassion for suffering and commitment to absolving it in himself and others became his focus and his mission.

Maynard eventually became a judge and made it his goal to rehabilitate people rather than punish them. He sentenced addicts to treatment instead of to prison. He donated his time and his resources to the Wounded Warrior Project. Maynard continued therapy and attended meetings, and developed compassion and serenity within himself. In his heart, he still feels that golden bond with his brother; his laugh still rings in his ears. This image that Maynard visualized overpowered the traumatic images of loss, and replaced them with one of love and acceptance. He would utilize his grit and determination and would never give up on fighting for his recovery—and for the legacy of his brother.

~

EIGHT

ANIMAL

IMAGINE A WORLD WITHOUT ANIMALS. Remove the birds from the sky, the squirrels from the trees, the whales from the ocean, the horses from the fields, and the dog from your lap. Imagine that the world consisted only of human beings—we creatures of angst and internal complexities. The world would be such a different place, absent the depth and meaning that animals bring to us. If not for the animals, who would remind us to slow down and play? Who would greet us at the door at the end of a long day with wagging tails and dancing eyes? Who would teach us about loyalty, tenderness, and nobility? Who would help to heal us when our hearts have been broken? Animals are fellow sojourners in this life, capable of tremendous connection and love.

In 1954, black-and-white televisions across the United States were tuned in to *Lassie*, featuring a rough collie and a boy named Jeff Miller, then later another boy named Timmy Martin. Lassie warmed the hearts of Americans as she courageously dashed toward peril to rescue her beloved boy and later to save other people and animals. The program, which aired for nineteen years, was the fourth longest-running TV show in American history. Lassie was best known for her keen abilities to perceive danger, rescue, and communicate with humans. The final scenes of each episode depicted a restored family and a child who had learned a valuable lesson. Lassie was the perfect dog, the ideal of a loving, intelligent, loyal, fearless canine who was uniquely bonded to humans.

History is rich with examples of animals, both real and fictional, sharing a unique bond with humans. Television, film, and social media are abuzz with animals from Scooby-Doo to Knut, the polar bear, to Marley, and the beloved beagle Snoopy. Producers and advertisers understand and capitalize on our love for animals, inviting them to play starring roles on commercials for products like beer, cars, and insurance. National commemorative days have been declared to honor and raise awareness about dogs, cats, horses, and other beloved creatures. Facebook pages and posts draw millions of views to read and see animal stories that delight us, inspire us, humor us, and awe us. A rough day can turn around in an instant by simply watching a YouTube video of a baby elephant blowing bubbles, or a talking dog. For some people, animals can save the day; for others, animals save lives.

Many people who survive trauma find refuge, strength, and healing through their bond with animals. Animals are beautiful and intelligent creatures. They are sensitive, capable of love, and exhibit a loyalty that is not often seen among humans. Animals walk beside us in quiet companionship, selflessly providing comfort, laughter, tenderness, and compassion. They teach us about safety and trust by being loyal, gentle, and protective.

A trauma survivor may have difficulty trusting people but is often able to develop a strong bond with an animal. A pet may provide them with a sense of emotional or physical safety that they have never before known. Many people in recovery from trauma claim that their pet kept them alive, provided them with a purpose, or taught them how to love. Veterans of war often find refuge from PTSD symptoms through relationship with a companion animal. Service dogs also provide support for those with profound emotional or physical disabilities. In trauma recovery, a person's ability to relate to and trust animals is indicative of a level of resilience capable of transforming pain into joy.

A traumatic experience is a personal violation in many ways: physically, emotionally, sexually, spiritually, or intellectually. This violation can impair a person's ability or willingness to fully trust or experience intimacy with others. This can happen when abuse occurs in childhood, or in a long-term relationship with another person. The abused person may begin to see the abuse as normal. They may begin to believe that they have no right to assert themselves. They may feel confused or receive conflicting messages from the person who abuses them. These kinds of struggles can distort a person's ability to trust appropriately or to recognize when a situation or person is unsafe for them.

When a relationship becomes abusive, it may begin in subtle ways, leaving the abused person to dismiss or make excuses for the abuser's behavior. Abuse may start with occasional angry tones that lead to shouting, name-calling, and disrespect over time. Sexual abuse may begin with intense emotional intimacy and secret-keeping, and then lead to greater violations. Physical abuse might be initiated by occasional pushing, grabbing, or intimidation, and escalate into continuous aggression and abuse. These types of trauma create a fracture within the person, leaving them feeling broken, worthless, and fearful.

Those who experience trauma may find it difficult to trust other people. They may interact with others on a surface level but never allow anyone to connect with their hearts. They may avoid being vulnerable and not let others know what they need or want. They may develop rigid rules about life and relationships that keep healthy people away, while invariably allowing the wrong people into their lives. This sets the stage for further trauma and heartache. Although this kind of self-protection is a normal response to pain, it can become a barrier to true healing.

Self-protection can take several forms. A person who is self-protecting may be guarded, suspicious of others, angry, and fearful. They may seem needy and desperately seek relationships with others, looking for someone to quell the painful wound inside of them. They may walk through life feeling numb and disconnected. Sadly, a person who is self-protecting may even have difficulty connecting with animals. They may disregard the value of an animal or see it as an inanimate object. Conversely, some individuals feel overly responsible to care for any animal they encounter. They may adopt many animals, sometimes allow them to breed, but be unable to care for them. Their house may be overrun with animals that are feral, malnourished, unvaccinated, and in poor health—often in far worse condition than if they hadn't taken them in.

If an individual can learn to care for an animal properly, they can learn to care for themselves as well. Animals teach us to be in the moment because they live in the moment, too. They remind us to return to the basics of breathing, sleeping, eating, peeing, pooping, and playing. They can bring us back to the moment with a playful pounce, a nudge from a wet nose, or a not-so-subtle demand to play ball with them.

Animals can also teach us about safety. Their ears listen, their eyes scan, and their noses smell. They remember, even for years, who is safe and kind and who is dangerous and threatening. They have the ability to react quickly when they are in danger. They can run, fly, bite, bark, swim, and scratch. A threatened animal can change the appearance of its body to look larger than it is. A dog that feels threatened may raise the hair on its back and bark loudly. A cat may arch its back and yowl as a defense. A pufferfish who is in danger can inflate its body with water or air and extend its prickly spine so that it is unpalatable to a predator.

Both domestic and wild animals provide us with examples of how to recognize danger, assert ourselves, and protect ourselves from harm.

Animals also teach us how to heal. When animals are wounded or afraid, they rely on their bodies' natural stress-response system to release the fear and pain until they can relax again, falling into a deep and comfortable sleep. A dog that is upset and afraid at a vet visit can wag its tail and enjoy a roll in the grass later that same day. Animals don't typically hold on to stress; they teach us what it means to let go.

Like humans, animals can also be traumatized. A domestic animal who has suffered abuse may have trouble trusting humans. They may be skittish or anxious around people or in certain situations. Most of these animals, however, are capable of healing. Many abused animals have successfully been rescued and restored from cruelty and abuse and are now fully incorporated into homes with families who love them. Although these animals often bear the physical scars of trauma, with caring and time they become active, happy, and loving.

Humans also have the capacity to heal from trauma. Individuals who experience trauma can heal in an environment of love, safety, and compassion. Often, humans and animals heal each other. Sometimes, the story of a human is analogous with the story of their beloved animal companion, allowing each to understand the unique challenges of healing that particular kind of pain. This kind of healing bond between animals and humans fosters resilience and hope.

"Until one has loved an animal, a part of one's soul remains unawakened."

—*Anatole France*

Lucy: Letting a Horse
Lead Her to Safety

Though she longs to erase it from her memory, it was a day Lucy will never forget. When she thinks of that day, her heart pounds in her chest, her throat goes dry, and she is filled with a shame that erodes every fiber of her self-esteem, leaving her feeling weak and hopeless. She tries desperately to shake the memory, but, like a broken movie reel, her brain plays the degrading scenes over and over again. The images are repulsive, ugly, and punishing, and she can't escape them. Like a vicious intruder, they invade her dreams, break her heart, and shatter her hope. Despite her attempts to overcome her past, Lucy is haunted by the memory of the day she was raped.

Before that happened, Lucy was a bright and happy person. She trusted easily, cared deeply, and lived fully. She loved to learn new things, enjoyed nature and animals, and openly shared her heart with her friends and family. Lucy worked as a physical therapy assistant and loved helping people heal from physical pain. She felt so much compassion for her patients who were hurting and celebrated their milestones of healing. In her spare time, Lucy volunteered at a no-kill animal shelter. Lucy took great pride caring for homeless animals and getting them ready to be adopted. She was thrilled each time she would see an adopted sign on a cage. She was also an avid horse-woman and had even ridden competitively when she was younger. Before the rape, Lucy loved her life and her work. Before the rape, she felt strong and brave. Before the rape, she felt she had a purpose. Now everything changed. Now she was different.

After the rape, Lucy spent her days and nights trying to erase the terrible memory of the things that had been done to her. Although she never enjoyed drinking, she began to buy bottles of wine and hard liquor. At night, she would start drinking until a warm, numb feeling encompassed her brain and body. She drank until she passed out and could sleep without being awakened by the nightmares that terrorized her. Sometimes, when she felt really frightened or ashamed, she would pinch or squeeze her arms or legs until it hurt. At times, she would leave bruises or marks on her skin that she would cover to hide them from her friends and family.

Lucy was disappearing and becoming a shell of someone she had once been. The only time she felt true relief was when she played with her dog, Charlie. Charlie was a beautiful mutt that she met and rescued while volunteering at the shelter. His pink nose and inquisitive brown eyes had won her heart. Charlie was her constant companion and they shared a special bond. Even now, Charlie seemed to sense her distress and stayed close to her side. He nuzzled against her and gently licked her hand, bringing her back to the moment and away from the darkness in her mind. She had saved Charlie from the cold and stressful environment of the shelter and now, it seemed, Charlie was trying to rescue her from this horrific nightmare.

Lucy felt numb and disconnected from herself as she stumbled through her days and drank herself to sleep most nights. Her thoughts tortured her as she replayed every detail of her relationship with the rapist. Like most victims of sexual assault, she blamed herself. She tells herself that she should have known, that she should have recognized the warning signs, that she is so very, very stupid. The negative monologue swirled in her mind over and over again. Lucy could not shake the belief that it was her fault.

To make matters worse, Lucy was terrified that others would find out and blame her for what happened on that dark night. Her rapist was not a stranger; her friends and family knew him, and they all thought he was a charming and kind man. They might never understand how he hid his darkness. She remembered a similar situation from her past when a girl from her high school revealed that she'd been raped by a popular football player. Sadly, it was the girl who was blamed and teased, compounding her suffering. Students cruelly taunted the girl, who seemed to shrink inside of herself as though she just wanted to become invisible. After her own experience, Lucy understood that feeling. She certainly didn't need to take on the blame of others when she had already blamed herself. She was terrified to be labeled "rape victim," fearing that no one would ever see her the same way again.

Lucy's rapist was her boyfriend, an older man that she had dated for six months. Early in the relationship, he seemed warm, attentive, and caring. Lucy found him attractive and enjoyed his attention. She appreciated the way that he held the door open for her or tucked a stray strand of hair behind her ear. He pampered her, bringing her flowers and cooking romantic dinners. She thought he had kind eyes and believed they were a reflection of his character. She loved the way he would call her at night to make sure that she was home safely. She thought he was so caring and protective. How could she have been so wrong?

In moments of clarity, Lucy realized that the red flags had been there all along. She mentally reviewed them during sleepless nights, hoping to sear the warning signs into her memory so that she might recognize them in the future. She mocked the innocent trust she had placed in her boyfriend and wasn't sure that she could ever trust anyone again. She even questioned the motives and behavior of family and friends, growing suspicious and paranoid that someone would hurt her again. Mostly, she didn't trust herself.

The first red flag was the night she caught her boyfriend driving around in her neighborhood, circling the building where she lived. She had been out for a run when she saw him driving slowly by, over and over again. Lucy tried to wave at him, but he sped up and didn't seem to notice her. Lucy thought this was strange, but when she confronted him about it the next day, he told her that he was looking for an address to a camera shop on her street. He claimed he didn't see her. She dismissed her worries because there really *was* a camera shop on her street. Later, though, she couldn't recall ever seeing him with a camera—did he even own one?

The second red flag was the time he sent her text messages that bordered on being inappropriate. She had been out with friends for dinner and a movie. He wanted to know where she had been and whom she was with all night. The texts were somewhat accusatory and demanding but with a hint of humor; he said he missed her and didn't want anyone else to steal her heart away. At the time, Lucy told herself that his jealousy was sweet and indicated that he really cared for her. She felt flattered and worked to reassure him of her affections. Still, after that, his jealousy increased and so did the need for reassurance. When Lucy would become annoyed or frustrated, he would simply remind her how much he cared for her. He would tell her that she was his everything. Looking back, Lucy recognizes how intense his jealousy had become. At times, she would provide him with a detailed account of her day to avoid his angry inquiries.

The third and final red flag was the night when she was spending time with him at his apartment. They were sipping wine and watching movies. She was enjoying his company as they joked and bantered playfully with each other. Within an hour, he began to make physical advances toward her that were aggressive and made her uncomfortable. When she tried to move away from him, he grabbed at her wrists and tried to force her to stay on the couch. When she asserted herself more strongly, he acquiesced and she moved away from him. Shaken and afraid, she made an excuse to leave his apartment and headed for the safety of her home and the companionship of her dog. Later, he called to apologize and sent her roses the next day. He said he had had too much to drink and felt overwhelmed by his feelings for her. He begged her forgiveness and promised never to do that again. Lucy was quick to forgive him, blaming herself for drinking too much wine and overreacting.

Even though she wanted to forgive him and move on, Lucy couldn't shake the feeling of fear and unease that settled in her heart that night in his apartment. Despite his jealousy, she really liked him and had even thought about a future with him. Now she was confused and cautious. Although he seemed to be caring and kind, she was beginning to see a different side of him—a side that frightened her. She decided to end the relationship, but she wanted to do it in person. She felt this was the right thing to do. She called him and set a time to meet. He said he would pick her up so they could go somewhere to talk. Despite Lucy's misgivings, she agreed to ride in his car.

That move proved to be a costly one for Lucy. She began the evening with the hope of an amicable discussion and polite agreement to end the relationship. She ended it bruised, beaten, and violated. When he picked her up, he insisted that they drive to a private area, somewhere away from the crowded café and busy streets. He drove for half an hour before parking in a darkened area, surrounded by large trees. Lucy tried to be kind and explain her desire to end their relationship, hoping he'd understand, but his anger seemed to explode and he turned on her, terrorizing her for hours. He threatened her, tortured her, beat her, and viciously raped her. She feared he would kill her and felt relieved when he finally drove her to a dark, dusty road where he tossed her brutalized body out of his car. He left her to stumble and crawl to safety, then she had to walk for an hour, bloody and beaten, before she flagged down a car to take her home. The driver offered to take her to the hospital, but she refused. She went home and stood under a steaming hot shower, trying to scrub away the shame. She survived the attack that night but was never the same.

Lucy never spoke to anyone about what happened to her. She willed herself to move on from her rape and lived in a state of denial. She tried to tell herself that it had been a bad dream, but the bruises on her face and neck belied this delusion. She called in sick to work and didn't answer her phone for three days. Later, when she returned to her job, she tried to cover her bruises in makeup and wore a long-sleeved shirt and pants. When someone noticed, she laughed and explained that she'd fallen while jogging. She blamed herself for what happened and tried to erase the memory of what he had done. She wanted her old life back, the life she had when she was in control.

Lucy struggled for months following her attack. She felt like she had lost herself and that she couldn't recall whom she'd even been before. She felt as though she were living a double life, lying on the outside to cover her tremendous shame on the inside. She was terrified that she would see her ex-boyfriend again. She was certain that she had seen his car driving down her street, but when she would look more closely, she would realize it was someone else. *Of course that wouldn't be him*, she thought, because he likely knew he had broken her so there would be no need follow her anymore. As the shell of the person she used to be, she wondered if this were true. She fought against this thought and determined that she wouldn't let him win. She would win, and she would heal from this pain.

Lucy knew she needed help; she couldn't do this on her own any longer. She read about a special type of counseling that involved horses, called equine therapy. Lucy felt drawn to this kind of approach because of her love for horses. Lucy believed that therapy was her last chance. If this didn't help her, nothing would. Since the rape, she had become concerned about her drinking and the amount of alcohol it took to bring her only temporary relief. Lucy was terrified of what she would say to a therapist. She hadn't breathed a word of her rape to anyone. She trembled at the thought of admitting all the terrible things that had been done to her.

The therapist was kind and compassionate as Lucy stumbled through her first few counseling sessions. Every time the conversation turned toward the rape, Lucy could feel herself shutting down, not wanting to relive the details. In those moments, her palms would become sweaty and her heart would race. She desperately wanted to be free from her pain, but the words were trapped inside and she was unable to speak. Her therapist suggested that she write her story down on paper, starting at the point where Lucy had lost her words—the night of the rape.

Although Lucy was afraid of putting her experience into words, she felt more comfortable writing about it than speaking it out loud. She wasn't sure how to pen the atrocities of what had been done to her. She became obsessive and critical of her words. She wadded up page after page and tossed them in the trash can, but finally, she stilled herself and began to write her story, word by word. Soon, the trickle of words turned into a flood. She allowed herself to cry as she wrote down the horrors of that night on paper. When she had finished, she sobbed and clung to her dog, Charley, with shaking hands. He quietly leaned against her, offering his love and loyalty, while she wept and grieved for all that she had lost.

She brought her story to her next appointment, not sure what to expect. Lucy was nervous but excited when the therapist met her at the door of the office and suggested that they would spend some time at the barn during this session. Lucy followed, clutching her notebook and blinking into the bright sunlight. She timidly followed the therapist down a winding path toward a barn. As Lucy glanced up from the path, she noticed a giant brown horse standing in a pen. The horse's eyes found hers and he whinnied his delight at her approach. Lucy broke into a smile. The therapist opened the door to the pen and invited Lucy inside.

Lucy took a seat on a padded chair in the pen next to her therapist, who watched for a sign that Lucy was ready to begin. After a few moments of silence, the therapist explained that they would spend the next hour together with the horse, named Bailey. The therapist talked about Bailey and his experience of neglect and trauma as a young horse. Lucy felt a kinship with this animal and a longing to trust him. She looked across the pen where Bailey stood and noticed how peaceful he seemed. The therapist explained how horses have keen instincts and can detect threats in the environment. She pointed out how Bailey's instincts told him that he was safe in the moment and could experience the peace that Lucy noticed. Lucy realized that she had not felt safe for a long time, and wondered if she would ever feel safe and at peace again.

After a few moments, the therapist asked Lucy if she wanted to share her story with Bailey. Lucy felt a quiet surge of panic as she glanced toward the horse standing in the distance, as though he could sense her dilemma. Lucy gathered her courage, opened her notebook, and began to read her story with a trembling voice. At first, she read the words in quick little gasps, refusing to make eye contact with the therapist. As she struggled to read, Bailey remained at a distance, seeming to allow her time. As the words poured from her, she began to connect with the pain that had been locked away in her heart all this time. Strangled sobs came from her throat as she read the most painful parts of her experiences—the parts where she had been violated and humiliated. At that moment, Bailey walked slowly toward her and moved to stand beside her. He nudged her hand with his soft nose and flicked his brown ears. She held her breath, afraid to interrupt this moment.

Lucy felt a deep sense of relief ebbing through her heart as she released all of the terror that had stifled her voice and stolen her hope. She allowed her tears to flow as she finished telling her story to herself, her therapist, and this horse. In that moment, she realized that she had survived, and that she could live again. She knew that her life would always carry the scars of her assault, but that she could love and trust again—these scars did not have to define her. Bailey taught her this in his quiet way. He reminded her that she could be safe and at peace if she wanted this for herself, and she did.

That day in the barn with Bailey changed Lucy. She realized that she no longer had to carry the weight of her assault alone. She had all the support she needed and wanted. She only needed to reach out for it. She began to tell her friends and family about her rape. She was welcomed with such love and kindness that it flooded her heart. With their support, Lucy decided to report her rape to the police. When she did this, she shifted the shame and guilt of her rape where it belonged, with her rapist. Regardless of the outcome, she could begin to live her life again and find freedom from the fear and shame that had held her hostage and nearly destroyed her.

Lucy continued therapy for several more months, exploring aspects of her story over and over again. Sometimes, her therapy sessions happened in the barn with Bailey and she would smile each time she saw him. At night, Lucy rested peacefully beside her dog, Charlie. She no longer felt afraid of the shadows and knew that she was finally safe. These two beautiful animals had walked beside her in her journey and taught her to love, trust, and to live again.

~

NINE

BODY

WE MAY CREATE DECEPTIVE COGNITIONS and rationales to justify our choices, but our bodies don't lie. Our bodies give us solid feedback, alert us to threats, require us to have limits, and provide us with boundaries. If we don't take the time to pay attention, our bodies *will* get our attention and will give us limits. Our bodies are such an incredible resource. Consider all of the opportunities our bodies give us every moment. The way our bodies respond and the potential for healing is truly miraculous. Often, we aren't fully aware of this capacity until we experience a loss, illness, or injury. The relationship we have with our bodies is one from which we cannot disconnect, even if we try. If we are more mindful of this relationship, and if we connect with our bodies with compassion, this connection creates safety, healing, and awareness of our natural resilience.

When a traumatic episode occurs, the stress of the event infiltrates the body. The lungs tighten making it difficult to breathe, nausea sets in, hands tremble, and stress and anxiety take over. After a traumatic experience, survivors often feel like their body no longer belongs to them. Instead, it becomes a slave to the stress cycles of hyperarousal and hypo-arousal. The body's natural response is to activate this stress response, to contend with the next threat, and take the option for either fight, flight, or freeze to survive. While this response is highly effective in the short term, it becomes exhausting and overwhelming, and leaves a person feeling depleted in the long run. Trauma survivors seeking an escape from this high-alert state may try to detach from their body. One of the most common methods of trying to disconnect from physical sensations is to check out and numb through chemicals, such as alcohol, which can eventually turn to alcoholism.

Survivors of sexual or violent trauma, in particular, may attempt to detach from the connection with their bodies. After such experiences, they perceive that it's no longer safe to feel emotions or to trust the embrace of others. Likewise, the body can become an enemy for a trauma survivor; rather than a natural part of them, it is now like a separate entity and a source of discomfort. Survivors often tell themselves shameful messages like, *I'm damaged, I'm dirty, I deserve pain,* which can translate into self-inflicting behaviors that cause even more pain. They engage in destructive behaviors like self-harm, binge eating or restricting food, or loss of emotional or sexual boundaries with others. The satisfaction or relief that can result from adopting these behaviors is the experience of regaining control. Control can become a powerful feeling for trauma survivors, especially when perpetrators have violated their bodies, stealing their sense of choice and control over their bodies and their lives. *Rapere,* the Latin root of the word rape, means "to steal."

The essence of resilience lives in us, and in our bodies. This is why one of the most important aspects of trauma healing is to reclaim our hearts, our narratives, and our bodies. By holding our bodies with unconditional love and respect, as if tenderly holding the child or infant part of ourselves, we form a compassionate connection with the body, and that gives us an opportunity to heal our wounds. This process takes time, attention, and patience. Simple practices like holding our hearts—a breathing technique that includes placing a hand over your heart and breathing in compassion—or simply breathing intentionally can bring us "back home" to ourselves and free us from the stress response.

As a trauma therapist, I facilitate body awareness and body-scan groups. During these sessions, I ask the group members to consider the relationship they have with their bodies. They share the messages that they give to their bodies, and also imagine giving voice to their bodies. It may sound like an odd question, but I'll ask, "If your body could speak, what would it say to you?" Once they start the process of imagining what their bodies might say to them, they open the door for reconnection.

There are many ways to reconnect with our bodies. For some, stillness and breathing techniques help reduce stressful feelings, and mindful meditation reconnects them to the physical. For others, connecting requires movement through dancing, hiking, walking, martial arts, yoga, or running. All of these options are ways to heal and connect, and allow the opportunity for self-expression through the physical body. Our bodies are our homes—vehicles that help us travel through our lives. When we return to the sanctuary of our physical bodies, we can connect with our resilience.

The following story is about Natalie, a woman who stays connected with her body even in the midst of devastating brutality. As she suffers experiences that are out of her control, she turns toward her body, her vehicle, and finds strength and courage to keep moving. Natalie finds safety within her physical connection that makes rational sense to her, while the rest of her experiences are confusing and painful. Through this connection, the only one that feels safe to her, she is able to survive violent trauma and transcend her experiences. This leads her to resilience and, finally, freedom.

"The body always leads us home . . .
if we can simply learn to trust sensation and stay
with it long enough for it to reveal appropriate
action, movement, insight, or feeling."

—*Pat Ogden*

Natalie: Her Body, Her Sanctuary

The trail she ran on so many times beckoned her. She crouched down to tie her Converse Chuck Taylor shoelaces in a triple knot because she didn't want to have to stop and break stride on the trail. Leaving her house helped her to get back home to the connection with her body, her breath, and a force she felt inside. She pumped her arms as her feet hit the sandy ground, sending dust clouds flying behind her. There was certainty in her steps; even through the crumbling rocks on the broken mesas she felt traction and confidence as she flew on her course.

As she exhaled more deeply, gaining speed, she felt fear leaving her lungs and her body. She understood the reasons for stress response, and she knew her option was consistently flight. She wasn't a fighter, and running felt natural for her, like she was built for it. Natalie felt like she had authority over the course of her life in those moments. She was choosing how to encounter her stress instead of her stress choosing her. As she moved through the desert, the energy of trauma became smaller and less influential over her thoughts. Each step felt like a movement toward her true self, her soul, and her body. She left the stress of her trauma behind her, in the footprint impressions that her Chuck Taylors left behind on the caliche floor.

Natalie spent much of her life tuning experiences out and shutting down, but when she was running she was tuning in and waking up. For many, this trail run would overwhelm, but Natalie welcomed the challenge. She felt inspired by her ability to run through the difficult terrain outside, and it also helped her process the emotional difficulties she experienced within. After she completed her usual loop, she would walk, cooling down, and sit on the same familiar rock, which was smooth and fairly comfortable. There she would breathe deeply and contemplate, preparing to reenter the stress of the cycles of abuse she encountered every day and night. As she exhaled, she focused on connecting with the softness and the strength of her body, embracing the soreness of her muscles, and relishing in the calm she felt in the animal part of her being. Soon, she would encase herself with the emotional armor that she required for protection from her family. As she blew out her last few exhales, she would intentionally detach from this precious and sacred connection with her body. She had to brace herself to walk through the door of her house and survive the night.

As a child, Natalie was often startled out of sleep by the crying and shrieking voices of her parents. She would cover her ears, hoping the sounds were just a nightmare, thrashing at her like torture, grating against her eardrums for an eternity until the noise finished with a crescendo of a loud crash. Sometimes she would hear soft cries, apologies, and whispers, and she hoped that meant they would go back to sleep. During these episodes Natalie would burrow into her bed, burying herself under her covers, her heart pounding, and perspiring with anxiety.

In the morning the house held a different reality. Her father cooked scrambled eggs and gingerly served coffee to her mother, who sat at the table with two black eyes. It was never a dream, although Natalie continued to wish that the nighttime noises were just a nightmare. As they kissed good-bye and her father left for work, both her parents seemed to be acting out roles of having a loving marriage, pretending the violence from the night before never occurred. Natalie's heart broke seeing her mother's bruised face. She wished she could do something to prevent the violence and protect her.

When Natalie asked her mother about it, she sharply dismissed her and responded angrily, saying that Natalie knew nothing about adult relationships, and that they worked it out. Her mother would then layer on makeup around her eyes, engaging in the errands of the day under a mask of denial. As a witness, Natalie absorbed all of the emotion that her mother was incapable of acknowledging or expressing. Though she had no bruises, she felt wounded by what she saw and heard, and felt complicit in the abuse. While she was in the house, she kept her mask on, too, holding back her tears and swallowing the words she was not allowed to utter. She waited until she went for her run, and as she moved, her mask and defenses would dissolve. While running, she connected to her own energy and authenticity. She exhaled and cried as she ran, feeling connected to her trusted vehicle. Her body never lied.

Outside, running on the broken mesas, confusion became clarity as she gained momentum on the trail and felt grounded in a reality of her choosing. Here she focused on her tangible, sensory experiences. The earth and her footprints were reliable and clear, unlike the swirl of dynamics she was living with in her parents' home. The trail she ran on was in close proximity to her house, but her movement took her far from the trauma that echoed through her mind and body. With each exhale, the image of her mother's bruised face began to fade, and the grating sound of screams faded from her eardrums.

The pattern of abuse was initially erratic but soon increased in frequency, becoming almost a nightly occurrence. Her father's anger gained momentum when her mother became pregnant with Natalie's twin brothers. Once, Natalie tried to intervene, begging her father to stop, but he pushed her away and her mother screamed, "Get out!" Her mother never fought back, or spoke about her feelings with Natalie. When Natalie tried to engage in conversation or try to help her, her mother would silence her, and remind her that this subject was off limits. She never understood why her father would hit her mother. He was caring and loving most of the time, but it was like a switch was flipped at night, and he had become a monster. Something about her mother's pregnancy seemed to set him off. When her twin brothers were born Natalie was filled with relief that they were healthy and came through the abuse in her mother's womb unscathed. Simultaneously, nausea filled her stomach as she realized what this meant. There was a sophistication in how he abused her mother, ensuring the babies would not be hurt—only her. The way he struck her mother was targeted and intentional; this pattern didn't change. However, he never laid a hand on the boys.

Natalie had difficulty sleeping and struggled at times with focus, but she still managed to excel academically, and joined the cross-country team where she could put her natural training into action. Her fashion staples were sweatpants, jeans, and her old faithful, Converse. She was becoming muscular from all of her runs, and she noticed the size and definition of her calves increasing. Her body was changing in other areas as well.

She had always been lean and muscular, but now she was becoming a woman. At first, she didn't mind the additional playful attention she received at school from her male friends, but sometimes the prolonged stares made her uncomfortable. Her relationship with her mother was already remote, but was now shifting into virtual silence with the occasional judgmental stare directed at Natalie. She felt significant hostility growing from her father. Suddenly, he began referring to her as a slut, and her mother would just nod in agreement. Natalie, mortified, could not understand how she had become a target. Her behaviors had not changed. She internalized the words and the judgment, and instead of feeling proud of her body she felt shame.

The tide was shifting in Natalie's family, and she was filled with fear and dread. Family dynamics were becoming reconstructed, and she felt like she and her mother were pawns on a chessboard with her father deciding where he would unload the abuse next. Natalie knew that she had already been moved into the position of becoming a target. Instead of the powerless witness of domestic violence, she felt the anger channeled toward her. She wasn't sure which position was worse. Natalie often thought that hearing the fighting and screams was more torturous than being abused. She pleaded with her mother, sometimes even with her eyes, unconsciously trying to align with her. Her mother was never responsive with Natalie, and their bonding was limited to her mother's directions for makeup application and a healthy skincare regimen. Sometimes, when Natalie looked into her mother's eyes, all she saw was vapid surrender.

Natalie felt trapped, like she was pinned down under a massive boulder that she couldn't budge. She often took on the role of peacemaker with her parents at the dinner table, negotiating through discord. She changed her twin brothers' diapers, read to them, and cooed over them, trying to relieve her mother and father from the demands of parenting. She excelled with high grades and was getting accolades for her athleticism. She downplayed her sexuality to avoid attention or humiliation from her parents and only engaged in mild flirtations. She completed household chores and was especially careful with her father's belongings, hoping he would notice these gestures and soften his anger toward her. She tried to console her mother and give her support, navigating around her perception of her mother's emotional needs. Still, none of these actions worked to prevent the anger and abuse.

The turbulent energy of violence continued between her parents. Natalie would also become pulled into the force of it despite her best efforts to rescue her mother and negotiate conflict. Thankfully, Natalie didn't have to worry about her brothers' safety; they were immune to their father's wrath. Natalie loved them deeply and felt almost maternal at times, even trying to teach them conflict resolution and ways to get along with each other. Although they may not have been targeted directly by her father they, like Natalie, heard the fighting and the violence at night. She hoped that they were not filled with the same fear and anxiety that she'd been living with. As they grew, Natalie noticed how their rough fighting became normalized as typical boy behavior. Their aggression increased and was encouraged. She began breaking up their physical fights, and sometimes they would even throw punches in her direction. The realization that she had no power over this storm of violence, not even with her little brothers, was demoralizing. Her efforts to love and help were met with disdain and anger. She retreated into herself, attempting to shrink so much that she would become virtually invisible.

While shrinking within her family system, she was also expanding and growing in strength and connection with her body. Her chest expanded as she inhaled and exhaled more deeply. When she ran, she didn't feel shame about her body; instead she felt strong, powerful, and capable of creating life force energy and connection. Moving in her body she felt like she *did* matter, like her thoughts and feelings could make a difference. She loved the ritual of running her usual path and finding her rock to rest on. Each time she completed her loop, she felt her endurance building and her speed increasing. The survivor within Natalie was gaining speed and momentum. With her cross-country team, she competed in races and individually outran all her competitors, becoming the state champion. The trauma at home didn't weaken Natalie. The irony was that her body was becoming physically stronger under the threat of humiliation and physical abuse. The bond that was developing between her mind and body became a dynamic force. Natalie knew that this relationship with her body could not be taken from her and was the safest relationship she had.

Natalie channeled her energies toward achievable aspirations. Because her efforts to help at home, were unwelcome, she focused on achievement outside of home where she would be validated and rewarded. She knew she was compensating for the lack of validation from her family, but how refreshing it was to be appreciated and seen for what she could do! Her teachers and coaches appreciated her talent, intelligence, and determination to succeed. The most important validation for Natalie happened in the quiet moments when she felt connected—mind, body, and spirit.

Natalie was offered both academic and athletic scholarships to college. As the months drew closer to her departure, she felt relief that the heaviness of the domestic violence could lift. She also felt ambivalence about leaving and worried that the abuse would become worse or her mother would suffer horribly with no intervention. As powerless as she felt, Natalie still assumed it was her responsibility to try and make a difference, and to stand guard in case something terrible happened, and she had to run for help. Eventually, she realized that in order to claim her own life and destiny, she would have to disentangle herself from this emotional responsibility and move on toward her goals. She accepted a full scholarship to a university, where she would run cross-country and track, and work on getting a medical degree.

Her parents were relieved that they didn't have to pay for college but never bothered to praise Natalie for this enormous accomplishment and her hard work. While this hurt, the finish line of this chapter of her life was approaching and Natalie couldn't help but feel relief. With high school graduation looming, when most of her fellow students were in the throes of "senioritis," Natalie threw herself into her studies, excited to take on the new challenges, in new environments, with different people and circumstances.

One night, she stayed up late to study for some of her final exams. She was exhausted and fell asleep on her bed, her desk light still on. Suddenly, a shock of pain went through her as she was awakened by a strong grip on top of her head. She was being dragged across the room by her hair, some of it being ripped out of her scalp by the ferociousness of the attack and the weight of her body. It was her father, screaming "Slut!" and "You just want to leave here so you can go be a slut!" The nightmarish attack continued as he dragged her by her hair into the living room and threw her against the wall. He started beating her with his fists. Sharp pain rang through her face and body. She tasted blood on her lip and one of her eyes was swollen shut, but with the other she could see him walk away. She hoped it was over. Instead, she could barely make out the outline of his silhouette moving toward her, gripping her brother's baseball bat. Standing over her legs, he raised the bat above his head, ready to unleash more of his brutal fury. Natalie crouched and turned to try to get away. Cornered with nowhere to go, she shuddered as she realized that she might never run again. Then she heard another voice coming through the darkness. It was her mother's, screaming, "*No!*" Her mother, who for years had accepted the abuse and never fought back, let out a primal scream to protect her. Stunned, her father dropped the bat and spun around. Natalie scrambled to get out of the corner and ran outside to her trail, spending that night curled up on her favorite rock.

She woke up shivering cold, with her mother looking over her stroking her hair saying softly, "I'm so sorry, baby." Natalie hoped the memories that flashed through her were a dream, but as she painfully strained to open only one eye she knew she had been beaten. Her mother helped her up off the rock, and guided her back down to the house. She'd never been nurturing and rarely touched Natalie, but now she held her every step along the path home. Her mother told her that she had called the police. After all the brutal beatings, this was the first time she'd ever done this. The authorities charged her father with domestic assault and took him to jail.

Back at the house, Natalie's mother tended to her daughter's cuts and bruises. She didn't cover them with makeup, as she had her own through the years. Instead, she acknowledged them and told Natalie, "This was never supposed to happen to you." She drew her a bath and carefully helped her into the tub. As her mother lifted her body, Natalie noticed the veins bulging in her mother's arms as if a new charge of energy was flowing through her bloodstream. It was as if a dormant strength had returned to her mother, and she was now present and back in her body. Natalie felt safe with her mother again, like when she was a baby, and relaxed into the water in the bathtub.

Natalie realized that her father had crossed a boundary with her mother. For some reason, her mother had accepted her own victimization, excusing and rationalizing it over and over again. She could tolerate seeing her own black eyes in the mirror, but seeing her daughter brutalized was more than she could stand. None of the justifications held. Although her mother never openly expressed appreciation for Natalie's running and athleticism, Natalie knew now how much pride and support her mother felt for her. Natalie felt washed over with the unconditional love from her mother that had never been expressed so openly before. She hoped desperately that her mother would also find unconditional love for herself.

Before Natalie left for college, her father apologized and said he was going to counseling. She wasn't sure if she believed him, but for now that was enough. Her parents' marriage would be their responsibility to sort out, and it was time for Natalie to move on. She would miss her little brothers, and felt love and concern for her mother, but now she was ready to live her own life. Hope carried her to her new home.

Her new trail became the track on campus at the university. She missed the jagged edges of her old trail at home, but she knew she would have to keep creating new paths as she transitioned through the different chapters of her life. She diligently worked hard to excel in her courses and on the track in races. Through the connection with her body, she found balance as well. She could slow down, soften, and contemplate, like she did on her favorite rock, and on her trail in the broken mesas.

Before her races on the track she would always bend down and triple-tie her shoes—no longer her cherished Converse Chuck Taylors, but instead, high-tech running shoes provided by the athletic program's sponsor. She loved feeling the pre-race adrenaline, hearing the sound of the gun going off, thinking through her strategy as she circled the track, pushing her body to its limits as she crossed the finish line to the roar of the crowd. When she realized she'd won her first college race, it was almost dreamlike. She was so focused and present in her body, concentrating on her breath and her cadence, that she was nearly unaware of her competitors. Just being here was enough. The act of running meant more to her than winning the race because, for Natalie, it was her lifeline—a natural survival mechanism.

As the crowd quieted down, Natalie looked up at the many faces in the stands. Then she locked on one that was most familiar. It was her mother, smiling wide with pride and affection, tears welling up in her eyes. She was surprised to see her. Natalie had spent the holidays with her roommate's family, and she had lost contact with her own family since she'd moved out. She didn't know what was happening with her parents; if they were together or divorcing. She no longer needed to know, or needed to rescue. Natalie had faith that her mother would find her own path, and it was time for Natalie to let go and claim her life. This was the prize that meant so much more than any medal: she had survived. Natalie knew that no matter what was to come, she would continue to cherish her trusted, sacred vehicle—her body. Whether she ran or not, and regardless of the stressors she would encounter, she would breathe and come back to her true home. Her sanctuary. Her body.

~

TEN

HUMOR

LAUGHTER AND HUMOR, LIKE THE SUN, are powerful forces that can change the forecasted outlook. Humor can change the way we see ourselves, and can help us to deal with difficult situations. It can help reestablish a connection to our heart and our spirituality, and can alter the chemistry of our brain and our body.

Humor and laughter are known to offer many benefits. It is thought that humor can reduce stress and improve overall health and wellness. Some research suggests that laughter may play a role in improved immune responses as well as providing some exercise benefit. Laughter is also a highly social activity, providing opportunities for people to connect to those around them. Laughter-focused services are a growing trend in our culture, such as laughter yoga or laughter therapy. This suggests that humor and laughter have the potential to support a meaningful recovery.

While some people may laugh easily and enjoy humorous moments, others may struggle to find their smile. Those who survive trauma are often plagued by depression and anxiety and may find it difficult to laugh. They may not see humor in their lives or may have trouble experiencing lightheartedness. Their brain chemistry may be altered from years of abuse or trauma, and they may struggle with the concept of happiness. Yet, there may be others who seem to laugh easily, despite their traumatic past. They may find humor in every situation and may see life from a humorous angle, in spite of their pain and suffering.

Some may speculate that someone who finds humor in painful circumstances may be using laughter as a defense mechanism. They may say that these people hide behind their smiles rather than show the world their pain. It may seem that their laughter is not genuine and may appear to be a form of stark denial rather than resilience. It brings to mind the image of the crying clown who wears brightly colored clothes and a painted-on smile, but cannot hide the tear that runs down his face. This type of humor is not resilience but rather a mask that hides pain and keeps true feelings and supportive people at bay. Humor that is used as a defense against pain only worsens the agony that lies underneath, keeping the persons forever trapped and just beyond the reach of recovery.

When a resilient person embraces humor, it stems from the reality of pain and the recognition of powerlessness. This type of humor is authentic and rich with wisdom. It flows from a person who is in touch with sadness and pain, yet refuses to surrender. It's a beautiful combination of wit and audacity, courage and hilarity. This type of humor provides a framework for understanding situations differently, and reduces the tendency to feel victimized by circumstances or people. Humor and laughter shift perspective and help to reduce the stress and tension that are the hallmark of PTSD symptoms.

Although some individuals are naturally humorous, others who tend to be more serious are nonetheless able to learn beneficial ways to use humor and laughter in recovery from trauma. The suggestion of humor does not trivialize the experience of trauma, nor does it negate the pain and suffering of the survivor. However, it does invite the possibility that we can live again after trauma. We can find our voice through laughter and dispel the belief that we are crushed or broken. We can embrace joy and the spirit of survival—and we can laugh.

> "Laughter is the sun that drives winter
> from the human face."
>
> —*Victor Hugo*

Sarah: Choosing Joy

Sarah's laughter is a hearty sound that is musical and resonant all at once. She answers her phone with a cheery "Hello!" offering both a greeting and a song for the caller. When people talk about her, they smile widely as they recall her kindness and her generosity. Sarah has the uncanny ability to find humor in everything, even the most painful of circumstances. Her light and laughter bring joy to all those who know her.

Sarah isn't the most educated person, yet she is intelligent and wise. She's not wealthy, yet she doesn't allow this to stifle her generosity. Sarah's most valuable assets are her children and grandchildren, and she delights in them as though they are precious gems. She takes a keen interest in their lives and has a way of making them feel special and important. She listens to them, shares from her heart, and tells them funny stories that they beg to be retold over and over again. These are often tales from her own childhood—early experiences of pain and sadness told through the lens of her own humor. Her warm laughter dispels her family's worries that she might have unhealed wounds from her life long ago. It's clear that wisdom has grown roots in her soul that stem from the scars of her painful childhood. What others see is her resilience and her strength—she is a survivor. Her children and grandchildren believe she is magic, that she can survive anything. Her past bears testament to that belief.

Born in 1944, Sarah was the third of nine children. Her father was an alcoholic, who drank away his weekly paychecks. Her mother was uneducated and often overwhelmed by the tasks of caring for so many people. As a small child, Sarah was poorly nourished, shabbily dressed, and fought for position among her eight siblings. Her mother made them meals of watery soup and stale bread, which provided little of the needed nourishment for growing children. Sarah can vividly recall the gnawing pain of hunger and the longing for something to fill her empty stomach.

From a young age, Sarah learned that her father was not a safe man. Perhaps it was an instinct as old as time—something born from the violent and drunken outbursts that he rained upon her mother during pregnancy. Likely it was because he hurt Sarah many times, teaching her young heart to dismiss him as a source of love or safety. Her earliest experiences taught her that he was capable of causing her pain and destroying the trust and hope that a daughter should have for her father. Mostly, she tried to avoid him when he drank. When she couldn't avoid him, she learned to cope with his abuse. She found safety in dark hallway closets, silently peeking through keyholes as he flew by in a rage. She learned to run fast and far down the street, her bare feet pounding on the sidewalk, her breath coming in short spurts. And despite her fear, she learned to find humor in the bleakest of moments and in the darkest of circumstances.

Sarah was most frightened by the times that her father would beat her mother. Her mother was her safe place and her source of life. Although a strong woman, her lack of education made her helplessly bound to her husband, unable to provide on her own for the needs of her nine children. It was always Sarah who tried to protect her mother from the cruel abuses of her father. When her father's drinking would escalate, she'd convince her mother to leave the house until he passed out. Sarah learned to anticipate her father's angry rages that often followed a long night of drinking at the local bar. She learned to calm and soothe her mother and her frightened siblings by making them laugh.

Although it would seem that alcohol ignited her father's anger, it was often periods of sobriety that revealed his darkness. He possessed an innate capacity for cruelty and seemed to take great pleasure in berating and belittling those around him. Sarah cannot ever recall any display of kindness or love from her father. She only remembers his irritability and anger. She recalls his quick, explosive temper, and the look of blind rage on his face as he came toward her. She remembers the beatings and how she felt like she was being consumed by the fiery blaze of anger reflected in his eyes. Those were the darkest times for Sarah. She felt like she had lost control of her safety and her ability to be happy. Those were the times when she would shut her eyes tightly and wish herself away into another world.

There seemed to be no end to her father's cruelty. This left Sarah in a constant state of anxiety and fear. Once, when Sarah was six or seven years old, her father asked her if she had ever seen a match burn twice. Not realizing what was to follow, Sarah shook her head no. She stood wide-eyed and fearful as he lit a match and blew it out. "There," he said. "It burned once." Then, he took the red-tipped match, still glowing with embers, and stuck it against her arm. As the match burned her tender skin, he said with a cold smile, "There, it burned twice." Sarah walked away from that moment with a burn on her arm and a scar on her heart. This incident solidified her belief that she could never trust her father. He had tricked her and played on her curiosity, something only a truly heartless person would do. In spite of his brutality, she willed herself not to close down and she kept her young heart open to the possibility of love and safety that existed within herself and others.

Sarah's father was notorious for drinking and driving, even while his children were in the car with him. On weekends, he would drive them out for a picnic by the lake. For most families, a picnic held the promise of a lazy, warm day of fishing, splashing in the water, and eating giant sandwiches and sliced watermelon. But for Sarah's family, these outings were fraught with fear as they watched a case of beer being loaded into the back of their rickety car. At the lake, while the children played near the water's edge, he'd drink the entire case. The children would eye him cautiously as the dark storm of his anger revealed itself first in the expressions on his face and in his eyes, and then roil up as he began to yell or curse. Eventually, his anger would be blotted out by the massive quantity of alcohol he had consumed, and he would begin to slur his words, slump to the ground, and then pass out. Sarah's mother didn't know how to drive and relied on her husband to drive them home. As day turned to cool night, Sarah's mother would have to wake him from his stupor so he could drive his frightened family home. At times, he would be angry at being awakened, and beat Sarah's mother with everyone watching.

In spite of the chaos and darkness in her home, Sarah loved school and enjoyed learning new things. The school environment was also structured and safe, providing a sense of normalcy and routine. Sarah also loved her warm and caring teachers, who may have recognized that her home life posed a threat to her well-being. Sarah spent many lunch hours with one teacher who often sent her to the store to buy ice cream for herself. It was a rare treat, and even years later she recalled the wonderful taste and sensations, and how it was like a healing balm for her fear and anxiety.

Sarah felt different from most of her peers at school. Although she tried her best, she could never afford to dress in the styles that the other, more fortunate, girls wore. Sarah often shared clothes with her sisters, which at least gave her a few more options than the two dresses that were her own. In spite of the challenges of poverty, Sarah was loved and respected by her classmates and friends, who appreciated her outlook on life. She was also known for her humor and, in middle school, was voted most likely to be a comedian by her peers.

As the storms continued at home, Sarah became more determined to escape. Although she loved her mother, she didn't comprehend her dilemma and why she chose to stay in an abusive marriage. She would often complain to her mother and beg her to leave. Her mother would only sigh and look away, changing the topic of conversation. Sarah was naïve and didn't understand how her mother's lack of education and financial dependency kept her locked in such a prison. She couldn't understand why her mother didn't just leave and take them all with her. In the 1950s, there were no support organizations or resources for abused women. Sarah's mother could have left them all, as some women did, and created a life for herself away from the abuse of her husband and the demands of mothering nine children, yet she chose to stay. She refused to abandon her children because her love for them was greater than her love for herself.

As Sarah grew older, she spent more time away from home. She often chose to stay overnight at friends' houses, relishing the quietness she found there. These times offered her a sense of peace and safety, which allowed her to find perspective. It offered her glimpses of a normal home life, which she determined to create for herself. When her father's anger left her feeling powerless and afraid, she was also often able to temporarily escape. These times helped her plan, and gave her hope that she could someday permanently escape the nightmare of violence and alcoholism at home.

When she turned eighteen, Sarah graduated from high school and left home for good. She was determined to create a new life for herself away from her angry father and the wake of poverty that followed his alcoholism. She rented an apartment from a family friend and worked at a restaurant to support herself. She was finally free and would never again live under her parents' roof. Although she missed her mother and siblings, she was proud of her life and her newfound freedom. She loved the ability to pay her own rent and buy her own groceries. Moreover, she loved having a quiet place where she could retreat at the end of the day—a place where her father couldn't reach her. In spite of her self-created solitude, Sarah was frequently awakened by terrifying nightmares. In her dreams, her father would chase her and beat her, or sometimes choke her. In every dream scenario, she saw the look of rage in his eyes and she could not get away. She wondered how long it would take before she would truly heal from the things he had done to her.

Sarah began dating a man that she met at her new job. He often frequented the restaurant where she worked as a waitress. Although Sarah had dated different boys in high school, she had never really fallen in love. But now, her young heart fluttered at the thought of her love for this man who was funny, smart, and handsome. At the age of twenty-one, Sarah married her young man with hopes and dreams of a different life than the one she had known.

Although they both loved one another, and had two beautiful children together, Sarah and her husband were unable to make their marriage work. Five years after they were married, they made the painful decision to divorce. Love didn't seem to be enough to carry them through their difficulties, or maybe they both were searching for something in the other person that they could not find. Regardless, Sarah never regretted the marriage because from it came her two beautiful children. She walked away from the relationship heartbroken but resolute; refusing to engage in self-pity and determined to move forward and pick up the shattered pieces of her dreams. There was no time to waste as she had two little ones who depended on her, and she needed to find a job and a home.

During those years as a single mom, Sarah did her best to provide a stable home for her son and daughter. She worked long hours in thankless jobs and struggled to make ends meet. She dreamed of going to college one day but knew that it was unlikely. Money was tight and she struggled to pay bills, but she made sure to provide her children with what they needed. She kept her sense of humor, even though she faced many lonely nights.

Sarah married for a second time, hoping to find someone to share her love and laughter. She was thrilled to learn that she was expecting another child. Although her pregnancy was normal, the delivery was marked with concerns for the baby's health and welfare. Later, when her baby was diagnosed with developmental disabilities, Sarah determined that she would provide her with the love and support she would require throughout her life. In spite of these ongoing difficulties, Sarah's laughter never faded, and she found humor in the daily struggles. She was often tired and she worried, but she refused to see life through the lens of her suffering. She saw self-pity as an anchor that would weigh her down, and she refused to give in.

Sarah worked to teach her children the valuable lessons she had learned through her own hardships. She taught them about kindness and the healing power of laughter. Her oldest daughter was a serious girl, often given to periods of somber reflection and anxiety. Her son was intelligent and sensitive but sometimes reckless, jumping his bike on homemade ramps in the street or being injured when playing with friends. Sarah worked to remind them of their potential and of the powerful opportunities that life handed them. She reminded them that they were smart and beautiful. She insisted that they stay in school and pursue the highest level of education possible. She connected to them with her heart, which revealed her incredible love for them. She tickled them when they were pouting, hugged them when they cried, and guided them when they were lost. She told them funny stories about her day, which would send them all into fits of laughter. She watched with great pride as her son and older daughter graduated from high school, college, and graduate school. She cheered and wept as her younger daughter received her high school diploma.

When Sarah's two older children married, she beamed with joy, and embraced her new family members as though they were her own children. When she became a grandmother, she happily took every opportunity to teach her grandchildren, and to hug and laugh with them. Her life felt complete and, as the matriarch of her family, she felt grateful that laughter and love prevailed. She was at peace, knowing that her grandchildren would never know the violence that had been the hallmark of her own childhood. She felt like she had come through a storm and could enjoy the tranquility on the other side.

But life has its twists and turns, and a period of good times can lull us into complacency, leaving us unprepared for the difficulties that await around the corner. Although Sarah had survived so much, she was to face yet another painful storm, one that would threaten to take everything away from her, including her life. She would need to rely on the strong foundation of her family and the bonds of love between them to survive.

In 2014, Sarah made an appointment to see the doctor after experiencing some troubling symptoms. In spite of her daughter's attempts to convince her to visit the doctor, Sarah had put it off for a long time. Although she cared so much for other people, Sarah had learned to minimize her own pain and suffering, to put it aside and move forward. Like so many people, she wanted to believe that cancer would never happen to her. Unfortunately, the doctor told Sarah that she had stage IV cancer. It had spread, and the prognosis for recovery was poor, sending shock waves of disbelief and fear rippling through her heart.

Sarah and her daughter stumbled out of the doctor's office that day and into the blinding sunshine. They sat wordlessly in the car, staring out the window at the cars passing by. The reality of her illness and bleak prognosis weighed them down heavily. They both knew that the days ahead were filled with very difficult things like surgery, hospitalizations, chemotherapy, radiation, oncologists, PET scans, grueling fatigue, and lots of medical bills. It was one of the darkest times in Sarah's life. She felt the familiar chill of fear and the sense that she was out of control, once again. Sarah wanted to scream and run away from the fear and uncertainty, to deny this terrible news and pretend it was a cruel joke. But this was her reality, and she couldn't escape it. She realized that she must be determined to do whatever it would take to survive. She loved her life and wasn't ready to leave it.

Sarah's family worried a lot about her during those early days after her diagnosis. They were afraid that she would crumble or decide to give up. They still did not fully recognize her resilience, something that would be revealed to them in the days to come. Sarah did not crumble, despite being afraid and discouraged by her diagnosis. Instead, she steeled herself against this intruder and quieted her soul for the battle ahead. She had worked hard to build the life she had and she was not going to throw in the towel so easily now. Like so many cancer survivors, her courage became larger than her fear. Cancer would not steal her hope nor would it stifle her laughter.

Sarah struggled in the difficult days that followed. She suffered through six months of chemotherapy that left her exhausted and weak. She underwent extensive surgery that required months of recuperation and caused significant alterations to her lifestyle. She survived three months of daily radiation that left her burned and fatigued. Although she allowed herself to be sad and worried, she also reminded herself to be courageous. She focused on the immediate task in front of her rather than the bigger picture. She chose to live in the very moment of her existence, rather than in the fear of her prognosis. Remarkably, she continued to share her melodious laughter with her children and grandchildren, giving them the gift of her joy in the midst of her incredible pain.

Two years later, despite the dire prognosis, Sarah is enjoying some time in remission. These days are a gift to her and to her grateful children. She fills her time with shopping, reading, taking care of her youngest daughter, and playing bingo. She loves her life and is grateful for these moments of hope and promise. She was told that she would not experience remission and that her lifespan would be shortened by this cruel disease. But she stands in the sunshine and breathes the air around her, recognizing the gift of her life. Although she struggles with the ramifications of chemotherapy and surgery, she finds humor in her life and in the reality of her struggles. She jokes about her limitations in funny, sometimes crass, ways. She lights up the hearts of those around her and reminds them that this life we live is a gift.

Sarah's laughter and her ability to find humor in things is evidence of her resilience. It's a trait that has been with her since she was a child, and one that she continues to nurture as an aging adult. It helped her to survive the darkness of her childhood and the looming threats of abuse from her father. It allowed her to find perspective when she faced divorce and the crippling loneliness that ensued. It became her anchor when the fear of cancer threatened to overtake her. Her humor is not a mask that she wears, allowing her to live in denial. She's real about her sadness and fear, talking openly about her past and her future. But humor has served to remind her and those around her that joy is always an option. She can choose to crumble or she can choose to laugh. I suspect that she will keep laughing.

~

ELEVEN

VULNERABILITY

VULNERABILITY IS THE SUSCEPTIBILITY TO be wounded or hurt. Most of us want to avoid being hurt or wounded by events or by others around us. In fact, we work hard to avoid it. We walk through life pretending that we don't care as much as we do, or we don't allow ourselves to hope, for fear of being disappointed. We may build walls in relationships so that others don't get close to us. We may push people away as we try to preempt being rejected. We're skilled at avoiding vulnerability because it exposes us to risks we may not want to take. We live in a world that often celebrates the strong and casts out those who appear to be vulnerable and weak. While we long for connection in our loneliness, we are unwilling to open the doors of our heart and expose our deepest longing for friendship or love.

Young children provide us with an excellent example of vulnerability. They are open without fully appreciating the risk of being hurt. They are clear about what they want and what they need. We know when they are hungry and when they want to play. They are also expressive about their dreams and aspirations as well as their desire for acceptance from others. They are comfortable with vulnerability because they have not yet experienced the menacing sting of disappointment or rejection. They foster a belief that their longings will be met with fulfillment.

Over time, however, children become less open and expressive. Instead, they learn to hide their feelings, to pretend away their wants and needs, and to limit their hopes and dreams. Sadly, they learn this when the world of reality crashes in and leaves them wounded.

Children or adults who experience trauma or profound loss may have even more difficulty being vulnerable with others. They may have built such a fierce wall of self-protection that it becomes difficult to let anyone in—ever. Deep hurt can leave tough, seemingly impenetrable, emotional scar tissue.

Resilience in recovery allows individuals to begin to take risks again, in spite of reminders about past hurt and disappointment. Many people confuse their vulnerability with the thing that caused them pain. They may believe that they are responsible for their own suffering because they were too open to others. Unfortunately, they may have difficulty understanding that their pain was caused by someone or something outside of their control. In truth, if we allow ourselves to be vulnerable, we are at risk for being hurt by someone else or by circumstances that we cannot always predict. We may walk away from people or experiences, promising ourselves that we will never trust again, never love again, never allow others to be close to us again. But deep within, we need to embrace the longing to try one more time.

We cannot spend our lives trying to protect ourselves from hurt by denying our hearts. True recovery allows us to embrace the risk of being hurt in exchange for the possibility of being deeply loved and accepted by others. When we can allow our hearts to break and refuse to close the door of hope, then we truly know what it means to live authentic and meaningful lives of recovery. Heartbreak and disappointment are inevitable, whether you experience them behind the closed doors of your heart or you allow them to manifest change within you. Heartbreak is not a punishment for being vulnerable. Heartbreak is an indicator that you allowed yourself to care, to love, and to live a life of meaning and purpose.

"What happens when people open their hearts?
They get better."

—*Haruki Murakami.*

Julie: The Strength of Vulnerability

The living room is decorated with pink balloons and streamers. Beautifully wrapped gifts adorn a table in the foyer of the house. Family and friends arrive in celebratory fashion, hugging the guest of honor and patting her rounded belly. Guests participate in games to estimate the size of the expectant mother's belly and try to guess the exact date of the baby's birth. Gifts are opened and tiny clothes are held up for all to see. Piles of diapers, crib sheets, rattles, and soft-smelling lotions all speak of the anticipated arrival of new life. For expectant parents, this is often a time of great joy and excitement. For Julie, however, these events are a painful reminder of the emptiness of her own womb; a deep and lonely void where the possibility of a child once lived.

Like many women who experience infertility, Julie has learned to live with the painful realization that she will never become a mother. She celebrates with her friends as they transition into motherhood. She hugs them and buys beautiful clothes that will be worn by their little ones. Julie knows that her friends care about her and are sensitive to the depth of her pain. She realized long ago that she was often the last one to learn of their pregnancies, not because her friends intended to leave her out, but because they saw and understood her sadness and her unfulfilled longing to be a mother. At first, she was hurt by this gesture, but she soon learned to accept it as just another loss associated with her chronic struggle with infertility.

Julie loved children. As a young girl, she often dreamed of being a mother. She had many dolls and took great pleasure in dressing them and feeding them with pretend bottles. As she grew older, she planned a career as a teacher and studied hard in high school and college. Her first day of work as a third-grade teacher brought her an immense sense of accomplishment and joy. Julie felt like it was the first step toward reaching the goals in her well-planned life. She loved teaching and watching each child in her class grow and learn so many new things. She found great meaning in being a part of a child's life, fueling their hopes and dreams for the future. She longed for the day when her own child would sit wide-eyed and wondrous in a classroom such as hers.

Julie met Lucas when she was twenty-six. They were introduced by mutual friends and quickly formed a strong connection. They enjoyed hiking and kayaking together, taking several trips to coastal areas where they could explore hidden coves. They would lunch together on the beach and snuggle on a blanket, watching the tide roll in and out. After a year of dating and friendship, Lucas proposed to Julie while on a trip to the Outer Banks of North Carolina. Julie felt like her heart would burst with joy and love for Lucas. They were married at sunset on a beach in Maui. Julie spent the following days of their honeymoon basking in the golden Hawaiian sun and the feeling that all her dreams were coming true. She married a wonderful man and soon they would plan to start a family.

Julie became pregnant within a few months after the wedding. Lucas was just as eager to start a family, so they were ecstatic to see a positive reading on the pregnancy test. Julie glowed as she imagined their future child and relished every moment of her new pregnancy. Julie excitedly called her friends and family and told them the good news. They all chattered happily and congratulated her on her pregnancy. Julie scheduled her first prenatal visit and began trying to estimate her due date. She and Lucas talked late into the evening about the baby and imagined who it would resemble the most. They fell asleep with the comfortable connectedness they had known since the beginning of their relationship.

Because she wasn't sure what to expect, it was easy to minimize the unusual pains in her belly that began two weeks after her positive pregnancy test. They were crampy pains that initially lasted for a few seconds but then seemed to intensify over the days that followed. Within a few days, Julie began to bleed, a possible sign that something was wrong. Julie cried as she Googled her symptoms and read that she could be experiencing a miscarriage. She refused to believe that she would lose her baby. She had dreamed of motherhood for so long that surely she would overcome this and have the baby that they already loved. Sadly, the pain and bleeding increased and the ensuing emergency visit confirmed their worst fears: Julie was having a miscarriage. The doctor shook his head as he performed a sonogram and could find no evidence that the pregnancy could continue. Julie felt as if her world had crumbled, and she cried throughout the drive home. She could not believe that her happy dream had turned in such a painful direction. She felt empty.

Julie grieved her loss in a private way, choosing to tell her friends and family about her miscarriage in an e-mail rather than by phone. She felt like she could not call them with this news. She didn't think she could find her words. She received so many supportive responses from her loved ones that allowed her to begin making contact with them in person. She was overwhelmed by their concern and love for her, allowing her to begin to move through her pain and find her hope again.

After her miscarriage, Julie held on to the hope that her doctor gave her, assuring her that she could try again soon and that early, first-trimester miscarriages were a fairly common occurrence. She embraced that hope, and she and Lucas were excited to learn that she was pregnant again three months later. This time, they decided to wait before they told anyone the good news. They were terrified of another miscarriage and didn't want friends and family to have to walk through that devastation with them again. Julie felt embarrassed to have shared the news of her first pregnancy with others so soon. This time, she held her secret close to her heart, like a delicate flower about to bloom.

Julie excitedly marked off the days on the calendar, estimating that she was now nine weeks pregnant. She was certain that she was no longer at risk of a miscarriage. She and Lucas planned to tell family and friends about the pregnancy when Julie entered her second trimester. Julie wanted to wait in case something had gone wrong. She was excited to start wearing maternity clothes and to see the gentle swell of her belly as her baby grew.

Lucas and Julie decided to celebrate the pregnancy with a trip to the Oregon coast. Although Julie didn't want to kayak, they planned to sit by the water and visit some of the surrounding towns. It had been a while since they had been away together. After the miscarriage, they both struggled with sadness and preferred to stay home together. Now, they excitedly boarded the plane, laughing at the families with small children, dreaming of how their own lives would change with the arrival of their baby.

An hour into the flight, Julie began to feel the familiar painful contractions that had signaled her previous miscarriage. She took a deep breath and tried to ignore the pain. She told herself it was anxiety or the movement of the plane. But with growing certainty, the pain became worse as they landed and collected their luggage. Julie was in tears when she went to the restroom to find she was once again bleeding. They left the airport and drove directly to the emergency room. Once again, they were given the devastating news that Julie was having a miscarriage.

Lucas and Julie spent the next several days in their hotel room. They were both in shock and deeply saddened by the loss of another pregnancy. They sat quietly through tasteless meals and made one attempt to walk on a nearby beach. Nothing seemed to penetrate the darkness of their moods, and they flew home two days early from their trip. There seemed to be a distance growing between Julie and Lucas, one filled with pain, longing, and disappointment. Once home, they both went their separate ways, trying to fill the void in their lives with busyness and noise.

Julie scheduled another appointment to see her doctor. She wanted to believe that modern medicine could help her cure the deficiency within her that caused her miscarriages. She wanted to be told that repeated miscarriages were still considered normal. Recently, she found herself questioning her role in the miscarriages, and wondered if she had done something to cause them. She often stayed up late into the night researching infertility and miscarriage websites on the Internet. She worried about her diet, her stress level, and exercise. She also worried that there might be something really wrong with her body that would prevent her from ever having a baby. She started following a diet she had discovered online that promised to create the perfect nutritional environment for pregnancy. She reduced her level of strenuous exercise and began taking dietary supplements. She read about basal body temperatures and ovulation cycles and even instructed Lucas about the right sex positions to increase the chances of pregnancy.

On the day of her doctor's appointment, Julie gathered her Internet research and her list of questions to take with her. She hoped Lucas would go with her to see the doctor, but he said he had an important meeting that he couldn't reschedule. He seemed dismissive of her worries about pregnancy and tried to reassure her that everything would resolve itself in time. Julie desperately wanted him to be with her and longed for him to validate her concerns. She was angry about his apparent disinterest and they launched into an argument in which she questioned his commitment to starting a family.

Julie arrived at her appointment alone and in tears. She was relieved that her doctor was so kind and supportive, listening as she reviewed the research and asked several questions. He reassured her and referred her to an infertility specialist. He told her that many women who experienced multiple miscarriages were able to have babies. He examined her and told her that he could find no obvious problems. He ordered a panel of blood work to check her hormone levels. He suggested that Lucas be tested for abnormalities as well.

Julie left the doctor's office feeling hopeful and eager to share the news with Lucas. She felt guilty about their argument earlier that day. She truly loved Lucas and longed to rekindle their connection, one that seemed to run as deep as the ocean. It was startling to recognize how their loss and her fears could drive a wedge between them. Julie had read about couples whose marriages didn't survive miscarriage and infertility. Their losses and desires for a family were part of the bond they shared. She would not allow these current struggles, or the ones that might come, to take her marriage away from her.

Although Julie had scheduled an appointment with the infertility specialist, she was excited to learn that she would not need it. Her period was a week late and she secretly went to the store and bought a pregnancy test. She squealed to herself when a second pink line appeared on the indicator window of the test. She was pregnant once again. Later that night, she prepared a special dinner for Lucas where she told him the news. He beamed at her and then gathered her in his arms, where he held her for a long time.

Lucas and Julie were quietly excited about her pregnancy. They kept the news to themselves, as if to shield it from threat or exposure. During the weeks that followed, Julie carefully watched her diet and avoided strenuous exercises. She went to bed early each night and took prenatal vitamins. She went to her first prenatal visit and began to embrace the beautiful hope of her pregnancy. Her doctor congratulated her and reassured her that everything looked fine. She was cautiously optimistic a month later when she still bore all the telltale signs of a healthy pregnancy.

Although plagued with morning sickness, Julie was filled with a profound sense of joy. She endlessly observed her silhouette in the mirror, looking for changes in her body. She would unconsciously place her hand on her swelling belly, feeling connected to the life inside of her. She pinned a sonogram picture of the baby on the refrigerator door, the grainy image a promise of the life she carried inside of her. As the weeks turned into months, Julie felt a growing sense of relief about her pregnancy. She felt that she could relax and enjoy these moments of hope and bliss.

The reality of the pregnancy settled over the couple like a beautiful dream. Julie soon grew out of her clothes and proudly donned maternity clothing. The midterm sonogram revealed that the baby was a boy. He was stunning, and all indicators pointed to a healthy baby. Julie and Lucas spent hours discussing potential names and imagining who the baby might most resemble. Julie loved the swell of her belly, round and beautiful, growing like their hopes for their new baby.

Their friends and family hosted a baby shower for them, bringing beautiful gifts and treasures to honor the awaited little one. Julie truly glowed, as though a radiant light flowed from her, filling her heart with pure joy. She felt like her dream of motherhood was finally coming true. She counted the days until she could meet her baby face to face. She was eight months pregnant and felt ready to welcome her son into the world.

When Julie was thirty-four weeks pregnant, she awoke from a nap to a strange sensation: the absence of fetal movement. She was accustomed to the baby's frequent movements, kicking and rolling within her belly. The baby often seemed more active in the afternoon, so she was worried to find that her belly was still and motionless. She took her hand and rubbed her belly, thinking that perhaps the baby was napping. She caressed her skin and breathed deeply, waiting for the familiar feel of movement, but nothing happened. Julie felt the first flutter of fear in her heart, a subtle warning that something wasn't right with the baby. She got up from her bed and went to the kitchen for a cold glass of water.

Two hours after the she first noticed the stillness in her abdomen, Julie called her doctor. He directed her to the emergency women's care unit of the hospital. Lucas drove her there, neither one of them speaking much on the drive. He pulled into a parking spot and quickly helped her from the car. A nurse triaged her and immediately took her to a room for further examination. Julie watched nervously as the nurse attached a fetal monitor to her belly. Lucas looked down at the floor and tried to control his shaking hands.

As soon as the fetal monitor was attached, Julie knew something was wrong. She strained her ear, hoping to hear the flutter of her baby's heartbeat, but found there was only silence. The nurse readjusted the monitor and tried to reassure Julie and Lucas. But she couldn't hide the look of concern on her face as she left the room to find the doctor. Julie began to cry because she knew in her heart that something was very, very wrong.

Julie doesn't remember the exact sequence of events that occurred that night. It felt like she was watching an odd, abstract movie about someone else. She remembers the hushed tone that fell on the room where she lay upon a cool metal table. She remembers the look on the doctor's face as he scanned her belly with the sonogram transducer. She recalls the continued absence of movement in her belly and the words "fetus" and "deceased" whispered among the medical staff. Julie felt cold and numb, a feeling that drifted into her bones, making her question if she would ever feel warm again.

Later, Julie was rushed into a delivery room and labor was induced. With Lucas beside her, Julie went into labor, filled with a searing pain that seemed to etch itself into her soul. What should have been a time of anticipation and wonder was now a time of fear, dread, and sadness. In the span of ten hours, Julie was fully dilated and was required to push. She was exhausted and felt like something inside her own heart had died along with the baby. After twelve hours of labor, Julie delivered her deceased son, who was born with the umbilical cord wrapped around his tiny neck.

Julie and Lucas did not speak or look at each other those first few moments after the baby was delivered. Julie closed her eyes to the world that seemed to be spinning around her. It was a world that no longer held her son and it was a world from which she wanted to escape, if only for a while. She was given pain medications and she drifted off into a tortured and brief sleep while the doctors did their best to make her comfortable. The wide-eyed staff made arrangements for a room where Lucas and Julie could be alone with the baby. A social worker came by to see them, but Julie could not form the words she needed to say. Instead, she listened to the options proposed: funeral plans, cremation, and burial. Julie wanted to scream at her and tell her to go away. Instead, she closed her eyes and tried to ignore the gaping wound in her heart.

The heartbroken couple spent the next several hours cradling their son, who was a fair-skinned child with a head full of dark hair. He had a tiny upturned nose, the mirror image of Lucas, and eyes that were brown like the earth. Although Julie wanted to run from the pain she felt in that moment, she couldn't be pulled away. She committed his every feature to memory. They gave him the name they had so carefully chosen: Liam. Cradling his lifeless body was like holding a fragile bird that she knew she must set free. He no longer belonged to her. In the final moments before they took him away, she placed a gentle kiss upon his soft skin and said good-bye.

Julie and Lucas were different people from the two eager expectant parents who had entered. Although Julie was discharged two days later, it seemed like months or years since they had arrived there. Julie numbly climbed into the car, feeling the emptiness of her womb. She didn't know where to place her hands and she couldn't bear to look in the back of the car where the new infant car seat had so carefully been installed. They arrived home to a place that she struggled to recognize. She went into Liam's room and laid on the floor, curled up in a ball. She cried for a long time before she fell into a deep and dreamless sleep.

In the ten years that passed since that devastating scene, Julie was never able to conceive again. For a while, she and Lucas struggled to stay together, both of them feeling the aching void of their son. Julie blamed herself for Liam's death and feared that, underneath his polite assurances, Lucas blamed her, too. She blamed herself for her miscarriages and her inability to conceive again and she struggled to feel whole. She felt as though her body—designed to bear children—had betrayed her and she believed that she was somehow deficient. She felt distant from her friends and embarrassed to be with her family. She felt like she didn't really belong anywhere.

Then Julie was thrown a lifeline. As though by fate, she began meeting other people who were affected by infertility. A fellow teacher at work, who became a very dear friend, shared her own story of heartbreaking grief at never being able to have a child. Julie was invited to attend an infertility support group where she met others who shared her experience. Julie felt connected to other women for the first time in many years. She felt as though she had a tribe now, a group of other women who related to her feelings of sadness and self-blame. She began to share more of her story of loss. Although she had never spoken about Liam and the night of his birth, she began to share pieces of this story with her new friends.

Julie had always been open and trusting, but shut down after the loss of her baby. Now, she began to open up to old friends again, believing that they would understand her journey. As she allowed herself to be vulnerable with others, her pain began to shift. The sadness never truly left her, but she was able to function again. Julie also allowed herself to reconnect with Lucas. Like so many couples who face such trauma, a painful space had formed where Liam and the dreams for a family once lived. Together, they decided that they shared a love that was more powerful than the pain of their past. They began couples counseling and spent time talking through their sadness. Julie once again felt the spark of love that had ignited in her heart for Lucas long ago.

In her recovery from their traumatic loss, Julie began to find herself again. She reclaimed her love for being on the water and enjoyed kayaking trips to the coast with Lucas once again. She earned a certification as a white-water kayaking and canoeing instructor. One weekend a month, she volunteered her time for a program teaching disabled children to canoe. In this way, Julie began to invest herself again in the lives of children who needed her.

On a few occasions, Julie was invited to speak to her infertility support group. She wept openly as she shared the pain of her loss. She felt completely vulnerable in those moments, as though all of her needs, faults, and desires were laid bare before others. Strangely, she also felt a great sense of peace knowing that her heartbreak might help someone else heal from their pain. As she saw the tears reflected in the eyes of others, she truly understood the universality of loss. She was not alone in her suffering, in fact, she never really had been. She was surrounded by people who understood what it was like to be broken and what it meant to recover.

Although Julie felt that she was finally beginning to heal, she still felt a heavy sadness when she thought of Liam. She often wondered what his life would have been like. She felt robbed. She longed to know what his voice would have sounded like, as he grew and asked a million questions, all beginning with the word "why." She knew she would never forget him and that she would carry him with her in her heart forever.

On a cool and cloudless day in April, Lucas and Julie paddled their kayak through the waters of Jackson Lake in Grand Teton National Park in northwestern Wyoming. The sun warmed their backs as it rose above the mountain peaks around them into the crisp, clear blue sky. As their kayak glided through the water, Julie breathed in the cool air and relished the tranquility. She spotted a black-billed magpie who alighted on a low-lying tree branch nearby. His song filled the air for a moment, and then he flew away. Julie thought of Liam and his brief appearance in their lives. Although Julie had always felt cheated by his death, she now felt gratitude that she had been allowed to know him. She felt like Liam was finally set free and that she could appreciate her journey and the strength of her love.

Julie vowed to always be open to the possibility of love and connection. This is what had allowed her to love Liam so deeply in his brief time on earth. As the sun reflected off of the glistening waters, Julie said a silent prayer for him. Lucas seemed to know her thoughts and gently met her eyes. He took her hand and whispered, "Liam would have loved the water."

~

TWELVE

FORGIVENESS

FORGIVENESS IS THE WILLINGNESS TO LET GO of resentments and anger held against someone for a perceived wrongdoing. We're all required to forgive someone at some point in our lives. Sometimes we are willing to forgive and sometimes we are not. Sometimes it's too difficult to let go of the pain that was caused us and we build walls around our heart hoping to protect it from further harm and help it heal. Other times, we forgive too quickly without realizing the extent of the harm done by the actions of others. We're often willing to forgive in measure with the level of the wrong done. We can forgive a friend for being late to pick us up for a movie date. We can forgive our brother or sister for forgetting our birthday. But it becomes more difficult when we're called upon to forgive our spouse for an affair, or forgive our mother for drinking away the years of our childhood.

We often forgive others because we want to continue in a relationship with them. We may forgive them because we want them to like us and we want to appear gracious. At times, we forgive because we tell ourselves it is it is the right thing to do and because we have the capacity to forgive. Sometimes we think we have forgiven someone for something only to be reminded of the anger we still carry somewhere in our heart. This is not really forgiveness; this is an attempt to forget or pretend the pain away. True forgiveness doesn't allow us to hold on—it means that we let go.

We often hear the phrase "forgive and forget." Though well-meaning in its intent, this is an impossibility because we aren't truly capable of forgetting our wounds. This phrase also implies that we can forgive quickly. This is also impossible. True forgiveness is a process by which we honor the pain in the wound, and it takes time and being patient with ourselves and others. Forgiving quickly means we have avoided the process of exploring our pain. We cannot truly forgive ourselves or others unless we completely understand what we are forgiving. A lender would never forgive us of a debt without knowing the amount of money owed to them. In the same way, we need to know the depth and meaning of our wounds before they can truly heal.

While we recognize the need to forgive others, we may negate the fact that we need to forgive ourselves. This is often more difficult than the prospect of forgiving others for a grievous offense. People often believe that self-anger propels them toward making changes. They think that self-deprecation and chronic self-blame may hold them accountable and prevent them from making future mistakes. They may believe that they aren't deserving of forgiveness, but rather punishment. This belief may become the foundation for the relationship they have with themselves.

Self-forgiveness is as necessary to our recovery from trauma as forgiving others. We may need to forgive ourselves for years of self-abuse, for self-hatred, for self-doubt, or for failing to recognize our worth in value. Self-forgiveness changes the nature of the relationship we have with ourselves and allows us to become more accepting of our struggles as well as our strengths. It allows us to see our potential for recovery rather than our faults. In this way, forgiving others and forgiving ourselves allows us to practice self-compassion, and provides us with the opportunity to grow and develop into individuals who are authentic, compassionate, and loving.

> "The weak can never forgive.
> Forgiveness is the attribute of the strong."
>
> —*Mahatma Gandhi*

Marcus: Finding a Way Back Through Forgiveness

The clock above Marco's desk read 3:15 PM. He stared at the hands moving slowly and methodically across the clock face. He willed them to move faster, longing for his work day to be over. Marco was tired and he looked forward to the weekend. It had been a long and taxing week of meetings, business proposals, and late-night dinners aimed at acquiring new clients for his firm. He adjusted his tie and tried to refocus his attention on the file in front of him. The phone on his desk rang loudly, most likely a client. Marcus sighed and sat up straighter in his chair before answering. He felt a mild flutter of frustration when he heard the voice of his sixteen-year-old son, Chad—his daily after-school call to Marcus.

"Dad, when are you going to be home? I really need you to come home soon," he said.

Marcus tapped his pen nervously on his desk. *Tap. Tap. Tap.* He answered, "I'll be there a little later. I have a few more things to do. I have a really important client who needs some information sorted out. I'm glad you made it home from school. Why don't you make yourself a sandwich and do your homework?" Marcus waited for his son to answer but was stymied by the silence on the other end. "Chad? Are you there? Did you hear what I just said?"

Marcus waited, hearing his son breathing quietly on the other end of the phone. Finally, Chad said, "Okay, Dad. I hope you come home soon. I really need you." *Click.* His son hung up the receiver, leaving Marcus feeling torn between his commitment to his job and his responsibility for his son.

Marcus struggled with the demands of being a single parent. His ex-wife was a chronic alcoholic who had abandoned the family shortly after Chad's birth. Although he was brokenhearted when his wife left them, he was also relieved. In the wake of her departure, Marcus felt a sense of freedom from the chaos of her drinking, yet he realized how ill-prepared he was to care for his son alone. Looking back, he felt like he had stumbled through the last sixteen years of his life, trying desperately to provide for Chad. Fortunately, his dedication and commitment to his job had provided him with some financial stability. This gave Marcus a sense of pride and he hoped that he could provide Chad with certain material benefits as a token of his love. Although he really loved Chad, he never felt comfortable sharing his feelings with him. As a result, he always felt like his son was somewhere just out of reach.

Lately, Marcus noticed that Chad had become more solemn and withdrawn, spending long hours holed up in his room alone. Marcus knew he should spend more time with him but he didn't know what to say or how to act. In truth, he just couldn't bear to see the ache and emptiness in Chad's eyes, a reflection of his own sorrow at the absence of the mother and wife who should be there to share in their lives. Marcus found that it was easier to stay busy at his job, where he knew the expectations and could control the outcomes, rather than at home where he could not find answers to the questions that seemed to haunt him. He preferred to flip through a client's file at work instead of trying to comprehend the internal world of his own son.

When the phone call ended, Marcus tried to shift his attention back to work. He cleared his throat and sat up a little straighter in his chair. But he couldn't seem to shake a growing sense of urgency to get home. Although Chad could be needy at times, he usually didn't seem as desperate as he had on the phone. Marcus rubbed his temples and stared at the file in front of him, wanting to finish the work that had seemed so important just a few moments ago. Despite his resolve to complete his work, his thoughts kept drifting back to his son. He got up and went to the copy machine to run a few copies of the documents from his file. When he returned to his desk, he picked up the phone and dialed his home number. He wanted to tell Chad that he would finish up early and head home soon. In truth, he was hoping the call would alleviate some of the guilt he felt about staying at work when his son needed him. *What did his son need anyway? What could be so important that he needed to rush home right away? Why couldn't he be more independent?* He wrestled with his thoughts while he listened for a connection on his phone.

The phone rang at his home without answer. Marcus furrowed his brow, pushed the end button on his phone, and waited a moment. Why didn't his son answer the phone? Maybe he was in the bathroom or out in the backyard. He dialed the number again and waited anxiously while the phone rang and rang. Where was he? Why wasn't he picking up the phone? Marcus tried to swallow down the panic that was rising in his chest. His anxiety felt unreasonable—it didn't seem appropriate to the situation. He tried to rationalize all the reasons why Chad wasn't answering the phone, but a deep sense of nagging dread began to tug at him and he knew that something was terribly wrong. He knew he had to go home immediately.

Marcus cleared his desk, ran to his car, and began the interminably long ride home. He couldn't seem to get there fast enough and pushed the gas pedal down a little closer to the floor. As he weaved in and out of traffic, Marcus tried his home number every few minutes from his cell phone but could not reach his son. He tried Chad's cell phone number but just got the voice mail saying he was unavailable. He called the next-door neighbors hoping they could check on his son but they weren't home from work. Marcus felt the cold dread in his heart as it turned in to a fear greater than he had ever known. He couldn't fathom why his son was not answering.

After what seemed like an eternity of traffic jams and stoplights, Marcus pulled into his driveway. The sun had set and a soft light emanated from the living room window of the house. Marcus felt a sense of relief—the house looked normal, undisturbed, quiet. He jumped from the car, slamming the door behind him and ran to the front door. He turned the key in the lock and stood in the doorway. He called out, "Chad? Chad, are you home?" The only answer was the panic-stricken echo of his own voice off the wood floors of his home. Marcus felt fear rising inside of him again. His feet felt like cement and he willed himself to move while he battled the looming feeling of fear and defeat.

He quickly walked through the house, hearing only his footsteps as he went from room to room looking for his son. Marcus kept expecting to find Chad asleep somewhere, wearing headphones on his ears, tuned out to the world around him. This was the only scenario that Marcus could imagine that would explain his son's silence. After checking all the rooms, Marcus turned his attention to the basement, the only remaining place in the house. He ran to the door and charged down the basement steps, calling out for his son.

Marcus was surprised by the cool dark of the basement. He hadn't been down there for quite some time, although he knew his son liked to spend time in the dank underworld of their home. Marcus wanted to believe Chad was okay but the feeling of dread increased with each descending stair. Midway down the staircase he paused for a moment, listening. He could only hear his breath and the soft hum of the refrigerator motor from the kitchen above the basement.

When Marcus reached the bottom of the steps, he looked around the half-lit room for any sign of his son. He froze in his steps when he spotted the outline of something hanging from the support beam on the ceiling. Marcus switched on the overhead light and saw the terrible image of his son: he had hanged himself with an extension cord. He uttered a deep and mournful roar at seeing his son's lifeless body hanging from the rafter. Marcus ran to him, hands trembling, and lifted his body upward, removing the cord from his neck. He laid him down on the cold cement floor and put his head down near Chad's face to listen for any sounds—a breath, a groan—but he was silent and unresponsive. Marcus grasped at his wrist and tried to find a pulse, but there was a stillness under his skin, evidence of a heart that stopped beating too soon. His shaky hands removed his cell phone from the clip on his waist. Through his tears, he called 911 and turned back to the blue and lifeless body of his son while he waited for help to arrive.

Standing in the hospital waiting room, Marcus dreaded hearing what he already knew. He tried to hold on to hope as he watched paramedics work tirelessly to try to resuscitate Chad. He told himself that his son was strong, that he was young, that he had potential. But deep inside he knew that he'd arrived too late. He sobbed, paced the floor, and waited. After a very long time, Marcus watched a young doctor walk toward him, his eyes somberly reflecting the terrible news. Later, Marcus was unable to recall the details of this conversation or how long they spoke. All that he could remember was that his son was gone. He'd been too late to save him.

In the days and weeks that followed the funeral, Marcus lived in a state of shock. The trauma of Chad's suicide left him numb and detached from everything around him. He felt crushed and paralyzed by a terrible sense of guilt that hung like a heavy weight around his neck. He couldn't sleep, he couldn't eat, and he constantly felt as though he couldn't breathe. He was haunted by the final phone call with his son. Marcus played it back in his mind over and over again. He tortured himself with each replay, remembering every word spoken, every tone, every sigh. The worst part for Marcus was remembering how irritated he felt with Chad, how he prioritized his work over his son's need for him. He had decided his work was more important than Chad, and now he was dead. He didn't show up for his son when he needed him the most. He would never get a chance to tell him he was sorry, that he mattered, or that everything would be okay. In his heart, Marcus believed that he had failed as a father and as a human being.

Marcus could not relieve the ache in his soul. He no longer found solace in work, his office serving only to be a place of painful memories. The clock above his desk seemed to mock him, ticking loudly as it marked the moments that separated Marcus from Chad. It was a reminder that he'd run out of time and was now condemned to spend the remainder of his life without his son. On his desk were pictures of Chad smiling in a baseball uniform when he was ten, and posing at the beach on a summer vacation two years ago. In the photo, Chad's eyes are alight at something he found humorous in the moment, his smile infectious and beckoning. Marcus couldn't look at the pictures without feeling like he was falling into a deep hole. Despite his determination, Marcus found that he was unable to work. He couldn't focus, and spent much of his day locked away in his office. He couldn't afford to quit his job so he decided to take a leave of absence. His friends told him that he needed to take some time to grieve and to heal.

But Marcus found that being away from work made everything worse. While his office proved to be full of painful memories, his house was even worse. There seemed to be so much evidence of his son's suffering—evidence he had ignored for such a long time. Chad's iPad was filled with music and games that spoke of darkness and depression. His room was chaotic and littered with books and dirty clothes. As Marcus stood to survey the room, which had once been a sanctuary for his son, he noticed a picture on the bedside table. Marcus walked into the room to look at the photo a little closer. It was a picture of Marcus's ex-wife, Chad's mother. Marcus picked up the photo and looked into her eyes. He felt such a piercing sadness that he returned the picture to the table, placing it upside down so he didn't have to be reminded of all he had lost. He closed the door to Chad's room and vowed he would never enter it again.

One night, Marcus found himself driving to the liquor store to get something to drink. He needed to calm his nerves and wanted to feel numb. He didn't really know any other way to take away the pain he felt in his soul. Marcus had never been a big drinker and would only partake occasionally when he was still married. He didn't want to replicate the ruin of his wife's alcoholism and had made a conscious decision to be sober. It had been many years since he'd had a drink, but in the face of such a painful loss Marcus felt like he had nothing left to lose. Now, he craved the burning fire of alcohol in his throat and stomach. He wanted to drown in a sea of liquor and find a place where it didn't hurt so much to exist.

Marcus opened a bottle of vodka on his way home and continued drinking into the night. In his empty house, he lay on his bed and cried for so long that his eyes swelled shut and his throat felt tight and hot. He cried for his wife, for his son, and for himself. He curled into a ball and wailed, painful broken sounds pouring out from him. He drank and he cried, never feeling as alone and hopeless as he did in that moment. At some point, he passed out and slept for many hours. He awoke at noon the following day, the sun streaming in his window, casting light and warmth upon his face.

Marcus stayed in his room for several days, alternately crying and drinking. He listened to music from his son's iPad—songs that spoke of loneliness and fear. As he listened to the music, he looked through his son's pictures and images. While most of them highlighted his pain and suffering, he also found several that reminded Marcus of whom his son was before depression began to strangle his heart. He found several funny pictures of Chad making faces at the camera or playing air guitar. He also found pictures of nature, the moon illuminating the sky at night, or a rare flower in bloom. Marcus was captivated by these images and how much his son had loved life. Marcus also found pictures of his ex-wife and son together. He couldn't remember when these had been taken but they were breathtaking. Chad was an infant, perhaps a few weeks old. His small face was nuzzled against his mother and she, in turn, looked peaceful and happy. She was stunning, a natural beauty who wore her caramel-colored hair cascading over her shoulders.

Marcus wished more than ever that he could turn back time and recapture this moment with his family. He wasn't in the picture with them, nor did it seem he had taken it. It seemed to Marcus that this described most of his adult life. He hadn't been in the picture with Chad. He had made his job a priority and had traded time with his son for the promise of a promotion and the hope of a raise. Marcus didn't think he would ever be able to forgive himself for making such a choice. He had been so unaware of the consequences of this decision—of how he would be left so empty-handed in the end.

His grief was like a roller-coaster ride. Although he continued to drink most evenings, he also began to take long walks through his neighborhood into other areas of town. He found that the walks helped him to clear his head and to breathe. He felt like he had been gasping for air for such a long time, unable to expand his lungs. In truth, he felt like his own heart had stopped beating the day Chad died. Since then, Marcus felt like he was living in some strange underworld where he was nameless and faceless, where he didn't belong. He felt lost without his son and he walked miles every day, hoping to find some way to navigate through this darkness that had invaded his life.

On one particular day, Marcus found himself walking in his old neighborhood, near his childhood home. He walked and searched the street names until he found the one he was looking for—Baker Street. Marcus turned down the street and continued walking until he saw the house. It looked so very small and it flooded him with memories. He sat down on the curb across the road and looked at the house for a long time. Marcus could feel a very young part of him stirring inside and memories dancing just around the edges of his mind.

Marcus closed his eyes and recalled himself at the age of seven, standing in the window, watching his father leave for work. His father, now deceased, had been a very successful businessman. He had worked long hours at his job, which allowed his family to enjoy the comforts of his financial gains. His father was always loving toward him, but was often gone from the home, leaving his mother to care for the daily needs of the family. Marcus remembered how he would get up early in the morning to have breakfast with his dad before he left for work. Although his father rarely spoke during their meals, Marcus believed that this was a special time and that his father appreciated those sparse moments together. Marcus was so proud of his father and wanted to emulate him. He dreamed of being a man who worked and provided for his family in the same way.

For the next few days, Marcus returned to his childhood home and sat on the same curb thinking of his own childhood and the legacy that had been left behind for him. He thought of his own father and the lessons he'd learned from him about life and the value of work. He remembered the sense of quiet desperation that he felt every time he watched his father walk out the front door of the home. He wanted to beg his father to stay with him—just a little bit longer. He wondered if Chad felt the same way when he left for work every day.

As the weeks went by, Marcus began to pull himself out of the deep hole into which he had fallen. Although he was still drinking, he began to have days where he didn't cry as often and where he felt more connected to his son. In the initial days after his son's death, he would cry out his name and question his life-ending decision. *Why? Why? Why?* was the refrain that constantly ran through his head. Over time, however, Marcus began to have longer conversations with his son. He began by talking with Chad about his day, usually as he took his lengthy walks around town. These conversations seemed to provide him with some relief from the agonizing pain in his heart. It was as though he could find a connection with his son and bridge the gap between life and death.

As Marcus continued to work through his sadness and loss, he began to see a counselor. It was not an easy decision for him and he dreaded the thought of pulling all his pain out for someone else to sort through in some sterile environment. But Marcus realized that he wanted to find answers for himself and perhaps a little relief. He wanted to stop drinking again and make decisions about the direction of his life.

Marcus made an appointment with a grief therapist, one he had seen advertised on the Internet. He dressed carefully and battled his nerves, finally deciding to have a drink before his appointment. With a few shots of vodka on board, Marcus walked the four miles to his first counseling appointment. He was unsure what to expect and was taken aback when he met the counselor. He was an older man, short of stature, and sporting a graying beard. He spoke with a New York accent, a mixture of brass and self-assurance. However, what Marcus was drawn to the most were his eyes—they were the kindest and warmest he had ever seen. His handshake was firm, yet comforting. He invited Marcus in, offering to walk through his pain and sorrow with him, and promising that he would find the courage he needed to heal.

Over the months that followed, Marcus began to explore his grief and sorrow in difficult and painful ways. At times, he wanted to escape and would be tempted to drink, but he managed to hold on to his newly established sobriety. Marcus found that his guilt soared to new heights when he drank because he felt it dishonored Chad's memory. He wanted to honor his son with the grief work he was doing in therapy, and felt that it was the only way to make amends for being the kind of father he had been—absent and disconnected.

Although Marcus carried a profound sense of self-blame for his son's death, he began to recognize that his role model for parenting—his own father—had been absent and disconnected as well. As a boy, Marcus idolized his father and looked for ways to connect with him. He had been so content to eat the emotional crumbs of his father's nods and limited interactions just to catch a glimpse of him before he went out the door each day. Marcus couldn't recall the exact moment that he stopped longing for connection with his father and just settled for what he was given. Over the years, he learned not to take risks or be vulnerable, but to embrace the value of work and productivity. With sadness, Marcus acknowledged how much he had become like his own father. As a parent, he had followed his father's example and, in doing so, he failed to be the father he should have been to his own son.

As Marcus put the pieces of his past together with the grief of the present, he began to feel a sense of acceptance and self-forgiveness. He gained new insights about himself and shared them in his conversations with his son. He began to write letters to Chad, opening his heart to the young man that never really knew him in life. He wrote to say he loved him, that he forgave him, and that he was truly so very sorry.

On a cool and windy day, Marcus visited the cemetery—a place that he had been unable to go in the months since Chad's death. He laid flowers at the headstone that bore his name and marked the brief span of time that his son had walked the earth. Marcus sat there quietly, beside the grave, and shared his heart with his son in ways that he had never done while he was alive. Although he shed tears for his loss, he also felt gratitude for his life and what Chad taught him. He knew that his son had left this world to be free of insurmountable pain. He prayed that Chad was at peace now, free of the darkness that had swallowed him. In his heart, he knew that Chad could forgive him and that their love for one another could not be separated, even by the finality of death. He knew that he could forgive himself and that this heavy weight of blame that he carried would slowly evolve into a sense of peace and acceptance.

As he prepared to leave the graveside, he felt an unusual sense of peace. For the first time in months, he felt like he could breathe. He inhaled and exhaled the cool air around him. He began to walk toward his car, remembering Chad's smile and the joy that he brought him. It was then that he began to believe that, although he was someone who was broken by life, he was also capable of healing.

～

THIRTEEN

COMPASSION

TRAUMA BREAKS OUR HEARTS. When a trauma occurs it actually feels like it rips a person apart, sometimes even taking away a person's ability to breathe and the will to live. The most important way to find healing after trauma is through heart connection, by beginning to breathe compassion back into our own hearts, and then becoming open to receiving compassion from others. Often with the most devastating losses, the only course of healing can be to find love again: not just the romantic notion of love, but also loving life again, loving moments and experiences, loving ourselves unconditionally and learning to be open to loving each other. Sometimes we need teachers to help us to learn how to love again. Our best teachers of how to love unconditionally are often our children and our animals, as the following story illustrates.

The definition of compassion is to suffer with, have sympathy for, and wish to relieve the suffering. Sometimes the meaning of compassion can be interchangeable with love, but compassion also encompasses a depth of understanding pain. Compassion is unlike avoidance or denial, it is a practice of becoming present with suffering and attuning to it with care. Many people with good intentions try to fix their friends or loved ones when they are suffering, offering statements like: "Don't cry." "Everything will be all right." "Cheer up!" "Don't think about it." "Soon you'll be back to your old self." While these statements may come from a place of caring, they minimize the pain and evidence a lack of tolerance for witnessing suffering. The more compassionate statement would show the willingness to be present with the pain of another person without judgment, with patience and understanding. Examples of compassionate statements are: "Take all the time you need." "It's okay to cry." "I feel your pain, you are not alone." "You have valid reasons to be hurting." "I'm here for you."

Often the most caring and compassionate thing to do is to validate the pain of another instead of trying to deny or avoid it. When it comes to our relationship with our self, and the meaning of self-compassion, the same definition applies. We cannot experience self-compassion if we avoid our pain, our trauma, our history of abuse or neglect. In order to have compassion for ourselves we have to hold our own wounding and attend to it, understand the suffering within, with the wish to relieve it.

Many clients I've worked with report that feeling compassion for others is much easier compared to having self-compassion. To truly be generous and giving to others, we must first have compassion for ourselves. Self-compassion is one of the most important practices for trauma healing and finding resilience.

In the following story, Mary grows up as an affluent child but with unstable, dysfunctional parents. She builds up walls and defenses and develops a dream of becoming a mother and having her own family. This dream helps her survive and gives her purpose. Unfortunately many of the patterns of the past follow her into her adult life. Mary is forced to address these patterns and face herself more honestly. She finds joy and fulfills her dream of creating a family of her own but also faces an unthinkable loss. The trauma she suffers forces her to question everything—including her own life. Through the depths of sorrow she discovers grace and compassion. With an opening for feelings of compassion Mary finds a reason to breathe and live again.

> "Love and compassion are necessities, not luxuries.
> Without them humanity cannot survive."
>
> —*Dalai Lama*

Mary: Compassion to Find New Dreams

Throughout Mary's life she was perceived as perfect and accomplished. She didn't require much attention, was motivated, self-sufficient and driven, even as a child, with a strong sense of purpose and clarity about her dreams and her destination. She parented herself. There was no other option with alcoholic parents who surrounded her with all of the comforts of affluence and abundance, but left her alone with the bare ache of emotional deprivation. Her radiant smile disguised her pain. She drove herself toward excellence in all arenas, achieved more than was expected of her, and maintained a near-impeccable appearance despite the hollow reality of her home life, and the loneliness of her internal, emotional world.

Mary never put her own needs first; she didn't know how. In her family she never felt seen or heard, so she neglected to see or understand herself. Her goals were focused on nurturing others, and building a world of love and connection where she could feel important and valuable. The dream of becoming a mother, and having a family of her own in her future adult life, gave her comfort and a reason to live. She fantasized about finding a loving husband and imagined holding her son or daughter, to whom she could give all the emotional support and nurturance that she'd never known or received herself.

This vision kept her going through the difficult times of her adolescence and early adulthood. Mary never strayed from her focus of actualizing this dream. She would be a natural because her first impulse was to nurture others and to attend to their needs and emotional worlds. She grew an uncanny ability to anticipate and read her environment, a skill that was finely attuned to growing up with two unstable, volatile parents who were perpetually intoxicated. Pleasing others, anticipating their moods and needs, became her gift. Mary grew up with no concept of feeling safe. For this reason, her emotional walls were erected and had become securely intact when she was a very young child. She hid behind these defenses so she would not feel hurt and neglected by her parents' constant drunkenness, and the painful reality that they both chose alcohol over their only child. She kept her heartbreak about her family locked away in a vault to which no one had access, even Mary. She maintained her presentation of perfection at all costs, never allowing anyone to really see her or her vulnerabilities. Sometimes, she felt like a cardboard cutout of a person, or a doll, built to fulfill the needs of others with no true core or anchor within.

Mary continued to cultivate her fantasy that originated when she was a little girl, alone and playing with her dolls, when she would act out the roles of her perfect family and her dream of becoming a mother. She would be the ultimate mother and would treat her child with boundless tenderness. This role of becoming a mother had been forming in Mary's heart for years, and she pretended to be a mother to her stuffed animals and her dolls, feeding them, grooming them, changing their diapers. This felt playful and normal for Mary and was a distraction from her lonely reality. In truth, Mary was a mother to real people before she fulfilled her dream of becoming a biological mother. For both of her parents she took on mothering tasks: cooking them meals, taking off their shoes, and even cleaning them up after they spilled, vomited, or urinated on themselves. Even though she was only a child, Mary took care of them like they were infants and had no choice but to accept the role-reversal of parenting her parents. She sometimes dissociated from the mess and remnants of the destructive style that they left behind. She performed functions beyond the role of a dutiful daughter, never complaining, keeping her thoughts and feelings inside—not that she had much choice, as a child she was powerless. *It was all worth it,* she thought, as this could be great preparation once she had her own family.

Mary finished prep school and then went on to college, where she continued to have a laser focus on finding a viable partner: a future husband and loving father who would be her partner in building her dream. Mary dated frequently with a clear criteria list for the candidates, who were often quickly dismissed, leaving them confused and befuddled. The traits she required in a partner were: high achieving, dependable, and definitely not alcoholic. Mary wanted desperately to start a family of her own, but she simultaneously feared that she could unconsciously replicate her own family of origin. She learned through reading many self-help books, and in her psychology classes, that people often attract partners who remind them of their primary caretakers. She vowed not to fall into this trap and thoroughly screened potential candidates on her many dates. During her junior year she found "the one." He represented everything that she was looking for: he was handsome, accomplished, and he didn't drink. She fell deeply in love with the safety, stability, and strength of their relationship. She hoped that together they would fulfill her dreams and provide fertile ground to heal the desolation of her childhood.

As Mary moved into married life she grew accustomed to the ritual of happy hour but with some trepidation, fearing that she'd succumb to alcoholism like her parents. She noticed how, after a first drink, she craved more. She figured that her genetic makeup was loaded for this sort of response, and harnessed her fierce discipline to fight it. She knew that she met all the criteria for an adult child of alcoholics, and was a true representation of codependency, but she knew no other way to live. Codependency served her in the respect that if she only focused on others' needs, and her external world, she would never have to face the pain in her own heart. She could hide from her insecurities, the raw ache of abandonment, remnants of her childhood that never left her. Mary compensated by displaying all the accoutrements of perfection: caring for others while secretly engaging in controlled drinking.

When the "plus" sign showed up on the home pregnancy test, and her doctor later confirmed the results, Mary experienced immense joy. After hearing her baby's powerful heartbeat she knew she would never feel alone again. Mary would later reflect on this moment as one of the happiest in her life. Her dream had been realized and the desire to drink any alcohol completely vanished. All the love Mary had, she flowed into Grace. Looking into her large brown eyes and holding her little hands gave Mary comfort and absolved her old pain. The nurturing she never received became attainable vicariously through their bond. She developed a new identity and a purpose as a mother, and reveled in the comfort of legacy, no longer fearing death.

For the first years of motherhood, Mary never touched alcohol. As little Grace grew and developed some autonomy, then left for pre-school, Mary returned to her happy-hour ritual, eventually loosening her one-drink rule. Her daily schedule revolved around Grace's needs and left no reserves of energy to devote to her marriage. As the months wore on, the volume of her drinking increased and the distance between Mary and her husband grew like a tide that receded but never returned. She couldn't identify precisely when the fracture began, but she knew the marriage had been breaking apart and was getting to a point where it might no longer be salvageable.

Mary had never been intimately close to anyone. She manifested her dream of creating a family, but she had no idea how to navigate through the next chapters of her fairy tale. She had no guide or template about how to develop partnership and intimacy through time. The one relationship that held clarity was the one with her daughter. Her love and energy for Grace was limitless, and she didn't need instructions when it came to parenting. The role of mother felt innate and natural for Mary.

Mary surrendered to the decay of her marriage, drowning her sadness in large glasses of Chardonnay. A new intimacy and partnership developed with drinking that became secondary only to mothering Grace. She tried to avoid this pitfall but she began to accept the inevitability that she would slip into alcoholism. As hard as she tried to fight against it, alcoholism became part of her destiny. She appreciated her husband for the security he provided for her and Grace, but beyond that she expected nothing except emotional distance. Her marriage dynamic became reminiscent of the pattern of abandonment of her childhood. Now, however, Mary knew that some of her choices contributed to this dynamic, unlike her childhood when she was powerless.

Mary noticed her husband's frequent, long business trips, and credit card receipts for places she'd never been. He often smelled of Chanel No. 5 (a perfume she didn't wear), cigarettes, and the sweat of another woman. She imagined there were numerous affairs since Grace was born. Mary hoped that her husband at least demonstrated discretion, decorum, and good taste in his infidelity. She couldn't blame him, and even felt relief when he gave up reaching across their bed. She could understand why he would extend himself in a different direction and reach out toward a more responsive partner.

After years of pretending, both Mary and her husband grew tired of holding up the façade of their marriage. They began to connect for the first time more deeply, not with sexual intimacy but with emotional honesty. They held their gaze longer together and were able to utter the words that had been hanging between them, the truth that their marriage was over. It was time to divorce and move on, they decided. When Mary and her husband sat down with Grace to tell her that they'd be living separately and would be getting a divorce, Grace clapped her hands.

Mary felt closer to her husband now after breaking out of this mold that didn't fit either one of them. She had accepted and even grieved the loss of her dream of a perfect nuclear family. She cared for her husband and wanted him to be happy, so she was able to release him along with her dream. Mary realized that the role of becoming a mother fulfilled and sustained her and was the most important part to her.

Both Mary and her husband transitioned seamlessly into their new roles as co-parents. They had been living as roommates for so long that the change didn't require much adjusting and offered breathing space for the two of them. Together, they laughed more, shared more, and relied on each other as friends and as partners in co-parenting. At first, Mary feared that communicating honestly would bring conflict but instead, through true dialogue, she and her husband had cleared a path for themselves that allowed for a more honest existence. There was more space now for compassion in the family.

This decision to become more honest and tolerant in such a fundamental way in her marriage forced Mary to question the honesty with herself, and her own self-care. This new awareness propelled Mary to make more changes in her life. She became more conscious of her need to maintain control, learned the limits of striving for perfection, and realized that this strategy she developed in childhood was keeping her trapped. Little by little, Mary started to open up parts of herself that she had previously tried to keep on lockdown. She decided to become honest with herself about her alcoholism and do something about it. She'd been so fearful of her parents' alcoholism because there was no end in sight. They were completely swallowed up by their drinking. Mary thought that she could be the one to change the pattern. She owed her recovery to herself, and decided that this was a vital step to maintain a healthy relationship with her daughter.

Mary started attending Alcoholics Anonymous meetings and embraced her single life by becoming braver and taking new chances. She began on the outside of groups and discussions, and sat quietly in the periphery of meetings, listening only, and collecting her chips. Mary knew that she needed to move into the center in meetings, and in her life in general. She starting taking more risks, and she began to open up and share. She found a sponsor and created meaningful bonds with others in recovery, making dear and deep friendships that gave her a new experience of community. As Grace grew up and moved into adolescence, their relationship became closer, opposite to what Mary heard from friends and others who struggled with teenage daughters. Mary also achieved her goal of providing for Grace what was never offered to her: consistent support, presence, understanding, and unconditional love from a parental figure. Grace received stability and love from both her parents even though they were no longer together. Pride and love filled Mary. She knew Grace was proud of her and, for the first time, she was proud of herself. She was finally taking down the walls that she had constructed from childhood, and learning how to connect and recover parts of herself and her heart.

The summer before Grace planned to leave for college, the family was struck by unbelievable tragedy. In the middle of the night, the doorbell rang and a police officer, with tears in the corner of his eyes, informed her that her daughter was in a car accident and didn't survive. Mary fell over, and shook with shock as her knees hit the floor, sobbing and screaming in pain. The police officer stayed with her and soon they were joined by her ex-husband and victim services. Mary couldn't focus and refused to believe this information was real. She kept rocking and saying, "No!"

Once Mary began to process the depth of this loss, she considered overdosing and taking her own life; overwhelmed with grief, she could barely make it through the day. Everything in her life now felt unnatural, nothing made sense anymore. With recovery, Mary had found clarity. Now she was lost again—her whole world had just been torn apart and taken from her. Her precious Grace was gone. She shut off from all the connections in her life, even from her friends and her sponsor. She returned to drinking more than ever, blacking out every day, hoping to black out this pain as she lost any reason to keep living.

Mary thought frequently of suicide, her heart ached so badly for Grace. She pondered about the afterlife and thought that perhaps she could be with her again if she took her life; she could be reunited with her in death. She even had a plan to overdose, and fantasized about experiencing relief and finally exiting this awful existence. In her sober moments, Mary felt extraordinary shame for relapsing, and realized that her drinking drove the pain of her grief deeper, causing the break in her heart to fracture further. Throughout the day she spoke to Grace, feeling grateful to be alone in these moments with no one to witness or to judge her and assess the level of her sanity. Mary felt like Grace could hear her and was responding, and frequently she felt a dialogue with Grace, not with words, but through movement in nature. The location where she felt Grace's presence the most was outside in her garden. Sometimes through the wind, or through the energy of a monarch wing, or through the flurry of a hummingbird flying past her, she could feel her daughter's presence.

Those moments gave Mary a lifeline as she wept for Grace. Mary remembered how Grace's smile broadened, and her eyes sparkled, when she found out her mother was working on the steps in recovery. Contemplating in her garden, Mary now began to consider, *What would Grace want*? When she answered this question to herself honestly, she knew what her daughter, now her angel, would want. She would want her to live, to find her recovery, and find love in her life. Mary's mind shifted toward earning the right to eventually join Grace, her angel in heaven.

Mary began to spend many hours of her day outside. As night fell, she would look up into the sky and see her beautiful daughter in the stars. She'd often fall asleep this way, in her chaise lounge under the light of the moon. These moments connected Mary with something greater, and helped her leave her suffering, even if for only a few moments. Under the influence of alcohol this spiritual connection with Grace was muddled, deadened, and interrupted. Mary recommitted to her sobriety and recovery, and reentered meetings now with a new purpose.

Her friends and sponsor were surprised to see her back in meetings, now moving toward the middle and sharing her story. Mary knew that she couldn't hide anymore; blocked, shut down, and living on the periphery was no longer going to work if she was going to survive. She began leading meetings, expressing herself, and sharing her grief.

As a perennial pragmatist, Mary knew that she needed additional support beyond her twelve-step meetings to face her grief. She needed to purge what felt like an endless flow of tears. She needed time, many hours, and many sessions and she also needed another presence; she couldn't live alone behind her walls anymore or she would die with grief. Mary needed a witness to stay with her and remind her that she wasn't alone. She began attending therapy for the first time in her life. Sometimes, she wouldn't speak at all for the full fifty minutes, weeping uncontrollably instead. Going through endless tissue boxes, she cried for her daughter, and for such an incredible loss. She cried for all the loss in her life: the lack of caring and the invisibility she felt as child; her inability to love fully and deeply in her marriage. Her tears came with the force of a dam bursting, gushing grief that had been repressed for years. Grace, the person she loved the most, had been taken, and yet it was Grace who taught her how to love. In therapy she found ways to honor Grace, and Mary committed not only to her recovery but also to becoming more open to love.

Through many sessions Mary practiced rituals to honor and celebrate Grace's life. On her birthdays she would release balloons in her daughter's favorite color combinations of white and pale yellow. The balloons were filled with messages of appreciation and love for the unending bond that Mary experienced. Mary kept reaching out for her daughter, writing to her, continuing to feel her. Simultaneously,

Mary felt Grace's presence guiding her through her grief and teaching her how to find grace, her namesake. On the anniversary of the accident Mary released paper lanterns in the night that rose up and glowed with the stars. Grace lit up the night, and along her path Mary felt her daughter's love and guidance. The opportunity to release and to reach out for her daughter was incredibly healing for Mary. The sadness didn't leave her, but through the crack in her heart a space was made for other emotions, including joy and incredible love for her daughter.

In therapy Mary learned about the importance of compassion, and how much it was lacking in her upbringing, and how she could provide some of this feeling for herself. Mary had been so deliberate and intentional with creating ideal external circumstances in her life, but she had never channeled her compassionate thoughts toward herself. She began to witness her life now from a bird's eye view, from an objective stance. When she could really see herself fully, without straining with exasperation, she could see a heroic woman who had been trying earnestly and desperately to be seen, to belong, and to feel loved. All the maternal energy that flowed through her now could come back to her. With the ethereal and spiritual support of her daughter, Mary learned how to mother herself, and she wrapped herself in the embrace of love she had been longing for ever since she was a child.

Mary moved through her life differently now; even walking her dog was a more joyful experience. One of her daily rituals was walking through the park with her dog, and then she would go to a neighborhood café where she'd have coffee and pastries. Her dog would also get his favorite biscuits—a satisfying trip for everyone. Walking meant more now for Mary. With the continual doses of compassion she gave herself, all of her senses were ignited. She treasured moments to feel awake and alive, and was open to her experiences. In the quaint café that she loved, there were other usual customers with their dogs, electronic devices, and reading materials. One customer seemed to time his arrival precisely at the same time as Mary's, and he also had a dog that loved to play with her dog. Mary was accustomed to keeping to herself and doing her own thing, but due to the boundless energy and playfulness of their dogs, she was obliged to engage in conversation. This unexpected dog playdate at the café became a daily ritual. The gentle fellow customer and dog owner became a companion. Their time together extended outside of the café. At first they would walk together through the park and linger at benches for hours, their dogs blissfully playing while the two of them shared and talked. Together, they ventured out on walks, at times without their dogs. They were both territorial, much like their canine pets that brought them together, and routinely returned to their favorite park bench.

There, Mary shared her story about the loneliness of her childhood, her distant marriage, the struggle of her alcoholism and recovery, and the joy of mothering Grace. She shared how she had never been vulnerable or emotionally available in any relationship except with her daughter. Mary spoke about the immense pain of her loss, and how she had been working diligently to honor Grace and to live her own life more fully. She told him that she was ready to be more vulnerable and open, but this was all new, unchartered emotional territory for her. They talked for so long that the afternoon turned to night. He listened as they gazed up at the stars. In that moment Mary felt held with love. She felt love for Grace as she looked up at the brilliant night; her daughter would always be with her in the stars. Mary felt love and compassion for herself for surviving, and growing, and opening her heart, and she felt trust and safety with her companion who showed her compassion. Mary could keep living for the opportunity to be alive and present for more moments like these.

Mary and her companion took their meetings beyond the park bench, and crossed the threshold into a commitment, which became the lifetime commitment of marriage. Although Mary had been married before, this felt like the first time she really opened her heart, and really committed to her new husband from the inside, instead of fulfilling a preconceived role like she did in her previous marriage. Her husband was divorced as well, and he was close to his children from his previous marriage. They were young adults but lived nearby and frequently spent time with him and Mary. Mary found unexpected joy in her marriage, with their new family of dogs, and with his kids who embraced Mary from the start.

Mary missed Grace every day, and continued to spend considerable time in nature and gazing at the stars with her husband, connecting spiritually with her daughter. She was overwhelmed with feelings of gratitude for the opportunities she allowed herself to live for, and for the compassion she received from her husband and his children. She had lost so much, but through surviving her grief she found compassion, she found herself, and she allowed her beautiful daughter Grace to teach her how to love again. Mary's dream as a little girl did not unfold perfectly as she imagined. Instead, she was granted a different life of enduring pain and grief, but by finding compassion and resilience she had the chance to breathe again, and live a different dream.

~

FOURTEEN

HOPE

"HOPE" SOUNDS WARM AND EASY. In reality, having hope is actually challenging and can also feel threatening. Hope asks us to look beyond our current circumstances, to understand the impermanence of the present moment, to imagine and reach for more. Hope requires expansive thinking, creativity, and the belief in internal strengths instead of external outcomes. Hope is having unconditional belief in ourselves, as the following quote from an unknown author describes: "A bird sitting on a tree is never afraid of the branch breaking, because her trust is not on the branch but on its own wings."

Sometimes, having hope means flying above the stress and struggle of trauma, if not in reality, then in our minds—having the ability to focus on our potential and the possibilities before they manifest into reality. Hope is an essential part of finding resilience. The essence of resilience requires energy and the capacity to leap and rise above what takes us down. The experience of trauma includes feeling trapped, inert, and powerless. Sometimes there is nowhere to turn, and no one to turn to. In these moments hope must be found in our hearts and in our minds. Accessing our creativity and the beauty of our imagination can become a lifeline in the midst of a tragedy.

THE ESSENCE OF RESILIENCE REQUIRES ENERGY AND THE CAPACITY TO LEAP, AND RISE ABOVE WHAT TAKES US DOWN.

There are times when hope seems unattainable for those under the pressure of loss and threat, and due to the fatigue of living in cycles of our stress response. Many who have normalized to chronic anxiety and depression find hope a foreign and disconcerting notion. It's frightening to let down, or to feel the sting of betrayal and loss after experiencing trauma. People often retreat to what is familiar because it can feel more secure, even if it's unhealthy or even life-threatening. Frequently, trauma survivors return to maladaptive coping methods because they know what the outcome will be. For a trauma survivor who has experienced powerlessness, finding control can not only feel corrective but can provide a sense of justice. This is the reason many turn to addictive processes, codependency, and isolation; the outcomes are reliable, habitual, and provide the *illusion* of power. Like a sure thing, these options can be gripped and leaned into like a security blanket.

Alternatively, hope is going "off the grid" with regard to comfort zones. Having hope is threatening because we have to rely on what we know in our hearts, even when we are full of questions or feelings of ambiguity, unsure about what might unfold in the next chapter of our lives. Turning toward hope and articulating our dreams takes courage.

This next story is about Rebecca, who grows up feeling like a misfit and is bullied and brutalized. Her ability to see beyond her present circumstances, and her belief in herself against the odds, saves her life. She finds solace in her imagination, fosters empathy for others, and through hope transcends her circumstances.

"Hope is a waking dream."

—*Aristotle*

Rebecca:
Hope for a New Chapter

From the time her fingers could turn the pages Rebecca was ready to read. Even as an infant she remembered cherishing the feel of the cloth toy books that were meant for chewing. Rebecca stared at the letters and the words, curious about the meaning, flow, and rhythm of them. She had soon graduated to Golden Books and then on to fairy tales and classics. The creases in the pages, and even the hint of mildew from the more dated, bound books, gave Rebecca a wonderful sense of comfort and held her like a prolonged embrace. She would imagine traveling into the stories, submerging herself into the context of the plots and becoming the characters.

Rebecca was drawn to the intrigue of fairy tales, but often felt compassion for the villain or identified more with the prince. Unlike many of her friends and classmates, she never related to the plight of the princess. The gowns and slippers and endless jewels and satin seemed tiresome and restrictive. Rebecca preferred to take on animal form for her childhood fantasies, or even become like a monster and experience an adventure with Max in *Where the Wild Things Are*. She identified with Huck Finn and imagined floating down the river on a great rafting trip with corncob pipe in hand, feeling completely independent and free. One book remained one of her favorite stories throughout the entirety of her life, *The Little Prince*. Rebecca loved the story and the adventures to all the planets, and she especially loved the wise words of the fox. She would often quote phrases from the creature, announcing frequently and loudly her favorite lines: "It is only with the heart that one can see rightly. What is essential is invisible to the eye."

The natural setting of Rebecca's upbringing in the suburbs of Seattle was calm and welcoming. The family lived along the shore surrounded by forests of ferns and endless views of placid water. But her family's energy did not reflect the comforting environment of their surroundings. Rebecca didn't see much of her parents due to the demands of their lives and their somewhat *laissez-faire* style of parenting. She felt curious about them and their stories. They always seemed distant, and attempting to draw them out or feel emotionally close to them felt futile. The warmth and depth of the characters in Rebecca's stories seemed more reliable and constant; they were always available, dependable, and would never leave her.

At a very young age, Rebecca was conscious of her quirks and her emotional sensitivity. There was a reason she repeated the quote from the fox in *The Little Prince*. She knew the tenderness of her own heart, and she searched for magic and love through her world of imagination because of the lack of nurturance in her family. In her life, she knew she would need backup and protection for her emotional vulnerabilities, and her favorite characters felt like her posse, whom she could call up in her time of need.

Many perceived Rebecca as possessing an unusual disposition and even a somewhat odd personality. Her teachers were often enthusiastic to work with her because of her creativity and the elasticity of her mind, but they otherwise never connected with her personally. Her parents recognized and appreciated her intelligence but when she'd come out of her room wearing mismatched socks and big, colorful hats, they'd roll their eyes, and ask her to change outfits before going out with them in public.

At age twelve, a budding adolescent, Rebecca wasn't imagining what seemed like her parents' perpetual cold snap of rejection. Hidden behind the newspaper, her father would peek around it occasionally to get a good look at his daughter, his glasses dropping down on the bridge of his nose, as he peered directly at her. She would smile, meeting his eyes with the hope of approval and grateful for the unusual opportunity to catch his gaze. His eyes would scan her up and down and then he would wince, frown, and sometimes even exhale with a disapproving nod. Rebecca felt his reaction like a blow. She'd shrink down, dropping her eyes to the floor, feeling defeated. She knew that if her father had his wish he would trade her up for a different daughter: one with flaxen, flowing hair who loved to dress up like a princess; a girl who could meet all his expectations of what a daughter should be, and could twirl around the kitchen laughing and dancing, performing for her father. Instead, he got Rebecca, who more often dressed up like a prince rather than a princess, who moved with an awkward gait and had spongy, unruly, red hair, best kept pinned back in a messy bun. Rebecca knew that she could never be the daughter her father hoped for, and figured it was useless to try to pretend otherwise. She accepted his disapproving looks and their distant relationship, and searched for approval through the magic of her imagination. Still, Rebecca couldn't avoid the encroaching feeling of sadness and depression. She felt like a misfit from the start, and often considered the possibility that there had been a mix-up in the hospital nursery and that she really belonged to a different family.

Her mother consumed her days with meetings and appointments and was in a constant state of business dealings. Rebecca felt perplexed by the demands of her mother's schedule and confused by the actual lack of productivity that resulted from her constant anxiety and hectic energy. Her mother's "uniform" consisted of matching sweater sets. She also ironed everything: her jeans, every tablecloth, napkin, or towel in their house. Even their sheets had to be pressed to perfection. Rebecca sensed that her mother would have taken the iron to her as well if she could—especially her hair. Rebecca's mother gave her several beauty tutorials at the mirrored vanity table in her room: clear guidance about using the round brush and/or opting for the flat iron to tame Rebecca's frizzy mane. Usually, after a considerable amount of time had passed, both Rebecca and her mother, drenched with sweat from the heat of the implements, surrendered. Even after all the pulling and scorching with the styling devices, Rebecca's hair would revert to its natural, frizzy state. Rather than trying to tame it, she'd pull it into a tight bun that would hide the texture.

Alone in her room, when she'd let her hair loose, she'd look back at her reflection with some approval. She could see beauty in herself that her parents couldn't. She even liked the dark green of her eyes and the unusual auburn tone of her hair color, how it bounced and held endless volume due to her tight curls. Rebecca also appreciated her personal style. She liked her array of quirky T-shirts, her collection of hats, and her unique flair for fashion. Rebecca took solace in her stories and the characters that she knew so well that became like chosen family members, and she imagined they would understand her in a way that her parents were incapable of. She desperately hoped that one day she would have living relationships that could rival the love she felt for her favorite characters in literature. Being an outcast was a sad, lonely existence. She hoped that one day she would be embraced for her individuality instead of rejected. She wished she could make these things happen, but she didn't know how.

Unfortunately for Rebecca, her misfit status followed her to school and elsewhere. She was mocked and bullied for her look and unwillingness to conform to the status quo. She fell back on her books and her imagination for protection. She rode her bike to school every day and—beyond the textbooks in her backpack—carried a bike basket full of other books. She hid behind them to avoid bringing attention to herself, and planned her route between classes to interact with as few people as possible. Rebecca had few friends and preferred keeping her distance. She spent time with a few teachers and had some study partners, but for the most part kept to herself. Rebecca had no concept of what a trusting relationship could be, and in general didn't feel safe with others. The only safety she experienced was through her beloved characters and the refuge of her own magical world that she created in her mind.

In her English literature class a very popular girl named Veronica seemed to take interest in her. She asked her to help her with her essays, was always impressed when Rebecca would read her writings in class, and noticed how she could elevate the classroom discussions with her eloquent responses to the teacher's questions. Rebecca thought it was strange how Veronica would stare at her in class, and sometimes she blushed because she felt awkward. One day after class Veronica asked if she could study with Rebecca and review their final essays for class together. Rebecca felt flattered that Veronica, such a popular and attractive person, would want to spend time with her. Rebecca thought that maybe Veronica could be a really great friend; maybe she felt awkward because no one had ever taken such an interest in her before. Rebecca decided that she would take a chance and trust Veronica, and maybe they would develop a meaningful friendship, and Rebecca could share some of her favorite stories with her.

That evening, Veronica came over to her house. Veronica was struggling with her paper and asked Rebecca to review it for her. As Rebecca was proofreading her essay, Veronica leaned over toward her and said, "You are so interesting," as she tucked one of Rebecca's curls behind her ear. Rebecca blushed, unsure of what was happening. Then Veronica leaned into her and smelled her hair and said, "Your hair smells really good."

A little taken aback, Rebecca stammered, "I use coconut oil to condition it."

Veronica laughed, *"Ha!* My mom uses coconut oil to cook with for its nutritional benefits." Then she leaned in closer and whispered in Rebecca's ear, "Let's see how it tastes," brushing her lips against Rebecca's earlobe. Suddenly, Veronica jumped up abruptly, exclaiming, "I have to go meet my boyfriend."

Rebecca, shocked and overwhelmed, jumped up with a feeling of warm relief. As Veronica ran out the door, Rebecca murmured, "See you next week in class."

The following week in class, Veronica completely ignored Rebecca as though she didn't exist. As Rebecca left the classroom she noticed Veronica congregating with a group of boys. One of them glared at her intensely, in a way that felt very threatening. Rebecca walked as fast as she could and almost ran out of the building. She heard a voice from the crowd yell out, "You weird freak, you better run!" From her peripheral vision it appeared that the group was following her. She hoped that her senses were deceiving her, and prayed that her fears were unwarranted while she headed straight for her bike. Maybe she only imagined the words. Still, inside her stomach she had a horrible feeling that this threat was very real and it wasn't over. The awful sickness in her gut led her to conclude that Veronica had betrayed her, and misconstrued what happened between them.

Rebecca's hands shook as she unlocked her bike and began to ride home as fast as she could. As she made it through her usual route and turned into an alley, the group of boys she had just seen in the hallway appeared around the corner in front of her. There were at least four of them, and they rode their dirt bikes toward her, then circled her like she was prey as they howled, "Slow down, freak! Creepy dyke, we just want to talk to you!" Rebecca felt so terrified she thought she might vomit. She looked at all her books in her bike basket. She wished she could escape by diving into one of her stories where everything was innocent and safe. She knew that a part of her did break off and dissociate in that moment, but a part of her had no choice—she was trapped.

Someone knocked Rebecca off her bike as they all laughed. Then they all punched and kicked her repeatedly as she lay on the ground. She forgot most of what happened next, but remembered the words "creep" and "freak" being shouted at her along with the laughter, spit, and the painful impact of the blows. One of the boys kicked her in the face repeatedly; the red swoosh of the Nike emblem on a shoe was all she could see. She crouched in the fetal position to protect herself but she'd been kicked so many times in the head she lost consciousness.

Hours later, disoriented and in pain, she became aware of her surroundings and what just took place. Her bike was twisted and wrecked like her body. Alone in the alley, she hurt so much and was in such shock that she was unable to cry. Eventually she somehow stumbled back home, walking her bike. She tried to hide the reality of what happened but the state of her bike and her body could not be disguised. Her parents were shocked at the sight of her, and never anticipated that Rebecca would be in a fight—they never considered she'd been in an unprovoked attack. Her parents put forth their best effort to help and asked many questions, but even after this horrible incident they still weren't able to console her or show her much warmth or compassion. They took her to the ER and made a police report. Rebecca was so terrified and shocked she could not give any description of the boys, all she could recall is that one wore Nike shoes with a red swoosh.

Rebecca's parents didn't know how they could keep their daughter safe at home, so they decided the best plan would be to send her away to a boarding school. They made arrangements for her to leave immediately, and were supported in their decision by their friends and Rebecca's primary-care physician. Rebecca, still in a state of shock and confusion, couldn't help but notice how rapidly her parents moved on this plan. It almost seemed like they wanted to expedite the empty-nest stage of their lives, relieved to unload their responsibility of caring for Rebecca.

Once the shock and the physical pain from that day subsided, Rebecca felt flooded with heartbreak and sadness. She cried so much her faced appeared red, bruised, and swollen for months after being assaulted in the alley. Rebecca felt more injured by the betrayal from Veronica than from the kicks and punches she endured in the alley. She had trusted her, and thought that Veronica genuinely appreciated her and her intellect. It was Veronica who had initiated the physical contact in her room, and now she felt used and betrayed, as if Veronica was acting out some secret, preplanned agenda. Rebecca felt ashamed and humiliated for opening herself up and trusting someone who clearly never cared for her.

The light and magic of Rebecca's imagination had been beaten out of her and left behind in the alley. Her curiosity and interest in reading became eclipsed by a dark self-hatred. Her favorite books collected dust, abandoned in her room as she went off to boarding school. In this new environment she felt socially ostracized even more than usual and sank into a deep depression. She rarely spoke in her classes and felt hopeless and despondent. Now when she looked at her reflection in the mirror she felt utter disgust with what she saw. She would often pound the glass with her hand and shout insults at herself, "Disgusting creep!"

Lonely and depressed, Rebecca found a physical place to retreat. It was a special nook tucked away in the library where she couldn't be bothered, and it became like a nest where she could cry without any witnesses. In the corner, she would curl up behind bookshelves in a pile of discarded beanbag chairs tossed in a corner. Sometimes she would just cry, hugging her knees, rocking for hours and wishing she had a way to escape her life and her loneliness. She often thought about ending her life, and even considered different suicide plans, going as far as the detailed note that she would leave for her parents explaining her reasons. Even in the depths of despair, she couldn't follow through. For some reason, a whisper of hope, like an unexpected character in her life story, reached out and connected with her, giving her a reason to live.

After shedding more tears than Rebecca thought was humanly possible, she had an epiphany—she felt a light inside of her, waking up in that corner in the library. The thoughts of self-hatred started to lift, and were replaced with a return to her childlike wonder. She started to believe that this pain could be fleeting and would pass, and her life could change and grow into something different. Like Huck Finn, she thought she could flow down the river and find a new adventure that was better than this. An incandescent and dusty ray of light came through the library window and provided comfortable warmth for Rebecca in her beanbag nest. She entertained a thought that maybe she *was* a freak, and would *always* be a freak. But she also considered that there might be other freaks out there, just like her, who felt equally as lonely and cast away, and maybe together they could create a tribe of freaks. Rebecca laughed out loud at this thought and felt a sliver of joy breaking up the heaviness of her depression. She felt peace in that moment, and for no tangible or plausible reason she also felt hope, almost like the warmth of the sunlight was delivering a message for her. She decided to hold on to this shred of hope and push through her pain, and began expressing the next chapter in her story through her photography, for which she developed a passion while completing her coursework in boarding school. Rebecca wanted to erase some of the lasting images that distressed her from the past, so she decided to create positive ones, and find new ways to share stories through a different medium—her pictures.

Rebecca eventually became a photographer and filmmaker and soon had websites and vlogs featuring her work. She mostly shared ideas and created stories about fictional characters. Rebecca still felt fearful about sharing her personal story, although she alluded to parts of her experiences through her photographs and videos. Four years after her attack, she considered that her creativity, her photography, and her wellness in general would be enhanced if she engaged in therapy.

Although she'd had many life challenges, Rebecca had never stepped into a therapy office before, and felt trepidation about the whole experience. Her therapist, who coincidentally had wild, curly red hair like Rebecca, welcomed her with a smile. She also shared the same appreciation for literature, film, and photography and would laugh out loud at her own jokes that were actually very ridiculous. Rebecca really liked her. Rebecca noticed how her therapist seemed free and celebrated herself. She wanted to "borrow" some of her vibe and learn how to discover this kind of joyful energy. During their sessions, for the first time in her life, Rebecca felt as if she didn't have to apologize for being herself. Trust started to grow, and the time spent there felt productive and even fun. Rebecca began to exhale and relax, and cautiously shared parts of her experiences. The lack of judgment she felt in her therapist's office helped to open doors within her self-expression that she never dared to open before.

Rebecca never spoke about her experience with Veronica or the assault. She felt so ashamed and confused about what occurred that she figured the best option would be to lock it up inside for good. As much as she tried, though, Rebecca couldn't completely forget about the betrayal and the pain of getting brutalized in the alley. Memories of it emerged unexpectedly and feelings of anxiety spiked along with her chronic experience of sadness and depression. She had long ago stopped using coconut oil to condition her hair because the scent nauseated her and reminded her of the confusion and betrayal she felt from Veronica. She felt scared when she thought that people in a group were making prolonged eye contact with her, and shivered with fear when she heard footsteps or sensed movement coming close behind her. Whenever she saw the swoosh of a Nike running shoe her heart pounded, and she felt sick sensations in her stomach like she was being kicked again. Then her head would suddenly pulsate with a headache. The popular logo that represents speed and motion, and in Greek mythology symbolized the flying goddess of victory, had the opposite effect on Rebecca. For her, the swoosh represented assault and violence, and just the sight of the emblem would send her straight back to the awful day in the alley. Because the brand had such popular commercial appeal, she was constantly being triggered.

Rebecca also felt incredible shame about the words that were shouted at her during the attack, and they still echoed in her ears, pounding her eardrums. It was like she was still being pummeled harder than the physical kicks with the words that were spoken with such vile hatred. Rebecca realized that she turned some of this hatred on herself in the subsequent months and years, calling herself those same words. Rebecca, a lifelong student of words and their meanings, was curious about why these terms were chosen for her, and if there was any credence or appropriateness to their application. Strangely, she didn't mind the word "freak." She even liked the term "super freak," and would play the song and dance to it with vigor, alone in her room. She could tolerate that one.

She did not feel the same way about "creepy." This word held disgust and repulsion, and made her sound like a troll or a voyeur, and Rebecca knew she was neither of these. She may have immersed herself in literature but she didn't consider herself nosy, and was certainly not interested in the gossip and drama of her peers.

In regard to Veronica, Rebecca knew that she was just the recipient of Veronica's choices and hidden agenda. Veronica was the one who pursued her, initiated contact and communication, buried her nose and mouth into Rebecca's hair, and rubbed up against her ear before she even had time to process what was happening. In reality, the word "creepy" was a much more accurate description of Veronica. While she was able intellectually to reject this ugly term that was spat on her in the alley that day, she didn't find it so easy to purge herself of the emotional imprint it had left. It bruised her heart and caused her to question herself.

With her therapist, she now had the opportunity to unload and release all of these thoughts and emotions that she'd been carrying for years. Rebecca began to nervously share her story in therapy, and once she expressed her voice it flowed from her. She spoke about not belonging in her family and how lonely and afraid she felt. She shared how her stories kept her from becoming enveloped in a dark depression. How the magic and transformation of the characters gave her hope that her life could change, too. Rebecca spoke about how much she wanted to feel a part of things, to connect in relationships, and attach to something as strongly as she felt attached to her stories.

For the first time, she shared how she felt with Veronica, how she felt affection and appreciation from another person, and how she trusted her. She also shared the experience of betrayal and the brutal assault she endured. She wept through her story, grabbing for more tissues as a deluge of tears and emotion poured out of her. Her therapist listened intently and supported Rebecca. Somehow, Rebecca felt as if her story held more meaning now that she was sharing it with a witness. The presence of her therapist felt comforting, even without her speaking, just the way she looked at her felt supportive. She explained to Rebecca that she had suffered traumatic experiences, and her symptoms after the assault were consistent with a diagnosis of post-traumatic stress disorder. Rebecca felt validated and vindicated. It made sense why she struggled with anxiety and depression and why she had such strong reactions to reminders of her assault.

Together with her therapist she worked on reclaiming her power and developing her own identity. Rebecca worked on desensitizing to some of the triggers and started by buying herself her own pair of Nike running shoes with a red swoosh. Rebecca wanted to embody and feel the energy of the flying goddess of victory. She felt like she could become heroic and powerful in the story of her own life, and could change the narrative about what that red Nike swoosh represented.

She imagined that with these shoes, she could rise up from the ground in that alley and fly away from the feelings of shame and humiliation. Her victory would be overcoming that trauma and finding new power to grow beyond it. Rebecca didn't want to be afraid anymore.

Rebecca worked on building relationships and joining communities with her therapist's support. She became an advocate and organizer, with the goal to reduce shame and judgment for those struggling with mental illness, and offered resources for those experiencing isolation and loneliness. She started a National Alliance on Mental Illness (NAMI) group in her community and was surprised by the turnout. The group grew to include many members struggling with depression, anxiety, trauma, and for those who never received a diagnosis but wanted to become a part of a community focused on healing. The group was supportive and fun and became a draw in the area. Rebecca would incorporate concepts that she had learned from her beloved characters in her favorite books, so the group could explore, create, learn, and grow together. Rebecca opened up through her vlog (blog with video) and drew many followers, especially after sharing her story about never belonging, and the brutal assault and trauma she survived. She wanted to create forums where people could congregate; people like her who felt like misfits, sentenced to an existence of isolation. What Rebecca grew to realize is that, through reaching out to others, she was also finding herself, honoring her own wounding, and discovering her voice.

Rebecca held on to hope as she continued to take risks, become vulnerable, and share her story. Rebecca shared her voice and created stories of empowerment about overcoming trauma and mental illness through her photos and films. She reclaimed her power and her potential to trust and lean into the support of relationships, now with many friends who shared Rebecca's journey and vision. Rebecca became a nationally known advocate and leader supporting those who have been victimized, assaulted, or bullied in their communities. She continued to develop more community organizations and outreach for those struggling; her goal was to reach out to all those who have felt discarded or judged for being different and help others share their stories in their own creative ways. She trusted her instincts and her heart as she moved through the challenges and welcomed new opportunities in her life. As much as she appreciated the visible and tangible expression of her art, her photographs, and films, she continued to hold on to hope for the future and for things she could not yet see. She would still say the words from the fox in the *Little Prince,* now quietly to herself: *It is only with the heart that one can see right. What is essential is invisible to the eye.*

~

Authors' Notes

From Kathleen

I WISH THAT I COULD PROMISE YOU A LIFE of beauty and peace. I wish I could guarantee that you would never be heartbroken again in this life. I wish that you would never know the shattering pain of loss or the devastation of betrayal. But this life is unpredictable, and we can't always choose our fate. People do not survive trauma by chance, but by the sheer force of the resilience that lives within them. While we are never promised ease and peace in our lives, we are equipped with the capacity to survive and to be triumphant over trauma. We can live again after we have been shattered. We are able to emerge from the rubble of our heartbreak and heal our deepest and most painful wounds.

My friends and colleagues told me that writing a book would not be easy. What they meant, but didn't say, was that writing a book about trauma would not be easy. They were right. Sharing stories about trauma and those who survive is not an easy task. It would have been easier to write happy stories of hope and joy, where there is only sunshine and there is never any pain. Unfortunately, those who suffered trauma would read those stories and turn away because they do not capture the struggle and suffering that characterize their experiences. This book is a testament of the cruel realities of trauma and the strength of the people who prevailed.

Trauma stories are hard stories to tell and painful to hear. We often want to turn away from the devastation of trauma, much like we would turn our eyes away from a frightening scene in a movie. In truth, we may fear that the end result will be more than we are able to handle. However, suffering can solidify our strengths and unveil, within us, a rugged beauty hewn from our most painful experiences. We cannot fully recognize that beauty unless we first walk through the pain. Character and strength are built from these struggles and we cannot bypass the development of these qualities. We must walk through the fire.

I often wonder if the human experience lends itself to trauma. In my practice as a clinician, I have met so many people who survived trauma and now stand on the other side, examining their wounds. As the world evolves and crises erupt around us, I suspect that most of us will experience a day or perhaps many days where our lives appear to be crumbling. Most of us will know the pain of trauma because we live in a world where violence, unpredictability, and chaos abound. Some of us will walk away from these events, shake the dust off, and attempt to return to our lives as we knew them. Others will suffer and will have difficulty coping with the sadness, shock, and anger that seem to have broken them. Like the people in our stories, everyone responds to trauma differently. Resilience is not only manifested in those who appear to be strong on the outside, it is also evident in the lives of those who suffer.

Suffering provides an opportunity to examine pain and to integrate it into the way that we understand ourselves. It allows us to develop a sense of meaning: why and how did I survive? Many of the people in our stories experienced a crisis in which they had to make a decision: *Do I want to recover?* The choice is never about whether or not we allow ourselves to feel pain or sadness. We must permit ourselves to feel emotions about our suffering. We can no longer silence our tears or our anger because they are a part of us. So often, a trauma survivor has learned to stifle their emotions because their experiences have been invalidated by those around them. They've learned to deny their feelings or to bury them deep within. But recovery allows room to feel and to understand pain and the significance of loss. Walking through painful emotions is often the crux of the crisis. Many people are stuck in the place where they shut down. Honoring pain and sadness while exploring the meaning of the trauma allows people to move forward into a new way of understanding themselves and others—with compassion and love. Resilience is found in the intersection between pain and hope.

Most of you who read this book have experienced trauma. My hope is that you can begin to examine your own life for evidence of resilience. You may think that you are not resilient and that you don't have the capacity to recover. Perhaps you've been lost in a cycle of self-destruction for a long time and are no longer able to separate what was done to you from what you have done to yourself. You may feel that you are broken or that you have no value. Those beliefs are only manifestations of the trauma and do not reflect the truth about you. If you survived trauma, you have resilience. You have resilience because you survived and because you are still searching for something to heal your wounds. Accept your resilience as a fact and embrace your strength.

There is no easy road to recovery from trauma. Realize that it will take time, support, and commitment. Many individuals find that therapy can be helpful in reducing PTSD symptoms and improving coping skills. Other people have found help and support in twelve-step or recovery-based programs. If you are struggling with profound symptoms of PTSD, consider more intensive forms of support, such as hospitalization or residential treatment. Many individuals with significant PTSD symptoms need the structure and safety provided in these environments, especially in early recovery. Please refer to the resource pages provided in this book for a listing of therapeutic approaches, online supports, and national resources available for those who experienced trauma. There is an abundance of help, hope, and support for those who still suffer. Recovery is not just a gift offered to some, it is offered to all who are willing to embrace their resilience.

FROM TANYA

Thank you for traveling through the journey of finding resilience with the brave trauma survivors in these stories. The hope in writing this book is that you, as the reader, would connect with them. We all have experiences to share and we all have resilience within us. If you are struggling or someone you care about is suffering, these narratives provide the opportunity to feel less alone, and to understand that there is the potential to find connection and resilience.

One of the many resources available in this book are steps for sharing a story of trauma. In addition, a list of resources has been provided for support for trauma healing, mental health services, and addiction and recovery services.

My hope is that these stories promote discussion and dialogue, and increase the potential for outreach and support for trauma survivors. Traumatic experiences, especially when they begin in childhood, have lasting effects on mental health and physical health in general. The effects of trauma are public health issues as well as mental health challenges. In time, if we create more opportunities to lift the stigma, remove the shame, and share our stories, then we also create opportunities that offer healing.

Working as a trauma therapist for decades has been an incredible inspiration. In the decades to come, I hope more people are included in the process of trauma healing, and have access to resources to discover the essence of their resilience.

CHAPTER DISCUSSION QUESTIONS

THE FOLLOWING QUESTIONS are designed to help readers share perspective about the characters and their stories. Use them for individual reflection, group discussion, in a book club, or in a clinical setting.

CHAPTER 1, STORY

Do you think learning traumatic information is as damaging as experiencing a trauma?

Do you consider an adoption traumatic?

Do you think Amanda's adoptive parents made a mistake by waiting to tell her the truth about her birth story?

Which part of Amanda's story do you believe helped her the most?

How do you think Amanda will tolerate intimacy in her future?

CHAPTER 2, SOURCE

Why did Henry keep his trauma a secret?

What do you think drove Henry to become a Marine?

What do you think was the most traumatic experience for Henry?

Do you think Henry was hurt more by the trauma from his mother's boyfriend, or by her turning an apparent blind eye to it?

What do you think was the most healing part of Henry's relationship with Stan?

CHAPTER 3, VOICE

In Chapter 3, Melissa seemed to have everything she could ever want. What do you think she was missing in her life?

Melissa was forced to attend a boarding school at a young age. Do you think there are benefits for a child living away from their parents at such an early age? Why might this be harmful?

As an adolescent, Melissa developed an eating disorder. What factors do you think may have contributed to this problem?

CHAPTER 4, TRUST

In Chapter 4, Jim is faced with the suicide of his father. Why do you think Jim thought of his father as a superhero after his death?

After his father died, Jim was haunted by the look of his father's eyes as he lay dying. What significance did his father's eyes hold for him?

Jim began to heal when he could place trust in others. Whom do you trust and why?

CHAPTER 5, RESPONSIBILITY

In Chapter 5, what did Naomi take responsibility for that caused her to feel guilty and ashamed?

In her adult life, Naomi loses contact with her parents. In terms of Jewish culture and family roles, how might this have become a significant source of sadness and loss for Naomi's parents?

Naomi suffered from generational trauma. How is this reflected in her views about herself and her struggles to have healthy relationships with men?

CHAPTER 6, GRATITUDE

Do you think Eliza would have found her resilience without her grandmother's apron?

What did you feel when you read about the abuse from Eliza's father?

Do you believe Eliza would have developed such a remarkable music talent if she hadn't survived her trauma?

How did you feel when Eliza moved out and left her father?

What creative expressions have been healing for you?

CHAPTER 7, GRIT

What does the term grit mean to you?

How did you expect Maynard to respond to his brother's death?

Do you think that Maynard should have been angry toward his brother?

What did you learn about PTSD from this chapter?

How do you think Maynard's parents survived their grief?

CHAPTER 8, ANIMAL

Lucy is nearly destroyed after a violent rape by someone she knew. Why do you think she didn't tell anyone about her assault right away?

Lucy engages in self-harm as a way of coping with her feelings of shame, anger, and fear. Have you ever engaged in something harmful to you as a way to cope with painful feelings?

Lucy has a powerful connection with animals that allows her to heal from her assault. Why do you think it was easier for her to trust an animal than to trust a person?

CHAPTER 9, BODY

Do you think Natalie would have survived her trauma without her ability to run?

Have you utilized your body as a resource during stressful times in your life?

How did you feel about Natalie's response to the abuse?

Do you think it is realistic that her father would actually apologize?

What do you think happened to Natalie and her mother's relationship after Natalie left for college?

CHAPTER 10, HUMOR

In Chapter 10, Sarah used humor and laughter to survive her father's abuse. In your opinion, what is the difference between appropriate humor and humor that is used as a defense mechanism?

Have you ever used humor to deflect a painful situation? If so, did you find it helpful?

Sarah survived many difficult scenarios in her life. Aside from her humor, what were other sources of her resilience?

CHAPTER 11, VULNERABILITY

Here Julie faced the traumatic loss of her unborn baby. In what ways did her pregnancy allow her to be vulnerable?

Julie and her husband, Lucas, experienced conflict in their relationship during their struggles with infertility and the loss of their unborn baby. Why do you think couples may be driven apart by these types of losses?

Julie is resilient because she allows herself to be vulnerable. Do you think vulnerability is a sign of resilience or weakness? Why?

Chapter 12, Forgiveness

Marcus is devastated by the suicide of his only son. Why does he blame himself for his son's death?

Suicide is one of the most difficult forms of loss that a person can experience. Have you experienced the loss of a loved one from a suicide? If so, how did you cope?

Have you ever been so depressed that you considered taking your own life? If so, how did your own resilience protect you from making that decision?

Chapter 13, Compassion

What do you think about Mary's childhood and her dream that came out of it?

How did you feel when Mary got divorced?

Could you understand Mary's experience of the loss of a dream?

How did you feel when Grace died?

Do you think Mary could ever realistically recover from losing Grace?

Chapter 14, Hope

How do you feel about Rebecca's character?

When reading about her assault, what did you experience?

How has your imagination and the feeling of hope served you in your life?

What stories or characters have given you hope or inspiration?

How do you think hope helps with finding resilience?

Steps for Sharing Your Story of Trauma and Resilience

Describe safe relationships, places, or experiences.

Identify the qualities in you that promote safety and resilience.

What felt traumatic for you?

How did you live with the traumatic feelings?

Which of your senses was impacted by the trauma?

How do you cope with stress response—fight/flight/freeze?

How does your trauma history impact your present experiences?

What did you learn about yourself from surviving the traumatic episode?

What qualities did you grow and develop as a result of the trauma?

What narrative or beliefs came out of the traumatic experience?

Can you describe a compassionate narrative about your survival story?

How can you connect with your five senses to feel safe?

Which quality of resilience in yourself are you most proud of?

What message would you give yourself if you could communicate with yourself during the age of the trauma?

How can you develop a more compassionate relationship with yourself?

What do you feel now that you have shared your story of trauma and resilience?

What message would you like to communicate to others about what you learned from sharing your story?

Trauma Recovery Resources

The following list provides an overview of the services and supports available to those who may be suffering from symptoms of unresolved trauma or related co-occurring disorders. This list is by no means exhaustive, but rather a representation of the most widely available community and Internet resources available.

Online Resources

The Internet is full of websites that offer information and resources for those suffering from PTSD or trauma related symptoms. It isn't possible to capture every Internet resource, but we have listed a few that might be helpful.

Aftertalk: *www.aftertalk.com*—This website provides online support to those suffering from grief related to the loss of a loved one, by allowing individuals an opportunity to express grief through writing. This site also features a question-and-answer forum to address grief related topics.

The Compassionate Friends: *https://www.compassionatefriends.org*—Grief education and support for those who have suffered the loss of a child.

Hope for Healing: *www.hopeforhealing.org*—Support, education, and resources for victims of rape and sexual assault.

Tragedy Assistance Program for Survivors: *www.taps.org*—Dedicated to providing support for those who have lost a loved one in active military service.

National Alliance on Mental Illness: *www.nami.org*—This website provides resources, support, and education for those suffering with mental health disorders.

PsychCentral: *www.psychcentral.com*—Has hundreds of online resources for individuals who experience symptoms of PTSD, trauma, addiction, and other mental-health disorders.

RAINN (Rape, Abuse, and Incest National Network): *www.rainn.org*—Information, resources, and support for survivors of rape, incest, and abuse and their families.

Ulifeline: *www.ulifeline.com*—Resources and education for college students with mental-health issues, trauma, or adjustment difficulties. The website also presents opportunities for users to locate local resources available in their area or at their university.

Mental Health America: *www.mentalhealthamerica.net*—Access to resources regarding mental-health recovery groups.

NCTSN (National Child Traumatic Stress Network): *www.nctsn.org*—Information and resources for families with children who have suffered traumatic grief or loss. The website also provides information and resources for children with parents who have served in the military.

Psychology Today: *www.therapists.psychologytoday.com*—This is a search engine to help users find individual, group, family, and marital therapists in their area in the United States and Canada.

The Substance Abuse and Mental Health Services Administration: *www.samhsa.gov*—This government website provides education and resources regarding substance abuse, trauma, and mental health disorders.

HelpGuide: *www.helpguide.org*—Education and resources for mental health disorders, substance abuse, and trauma recovery.

EMDR International Association: *www.emdria.org*—Information about EMDR and a search engine to locate a local EMDR provider.

Voices for Dignity: *www.voicesfordignity.com*—Education, support, and resources to those who survived sexual assault, childhood sexual abuse, sexual trafficking, and/or sexual violence.

American Red Cross: *redcross.org*—This organization provides a number of helpful resources for those who have experienced a natural disaster, as well as those serving in the military and for veterans. These include an emergency communications source for families.

RECOVERY SUPPORT GROUPS

MANY PEOPLE WHO EXPERIENCE TRAUMA struggle with substance abuse disorders or process addictions such as eating disorders, sexual addiction, compulsive spending, and/or gambling addiction. The following resources are available in most communities and can provide individuals with support, structure, and accountability in recovery.

Alcoholics Anonymous: *www.aa.org*—This website provides education and resources for those suffering from alcohol-use disorder, as well as access to local Alcoholics Anonymous 12-step meeting groups, locations, and times.

Narcotics Anonymous: *www.na.org*—This website provides education and resources for those with substance use disorders. It also provides access to listings of local Narcotics Anonymous 12-step groups.

Sex Addicts Anonymous: *www.saa-recovery.org*—This website provides education and support for those who are struggling with sexual addiction. It also provides access to listings of local Sex Addicts Anonymous groups.

Sex and Love Addicts Anonymous: *www.slaafws.org*—This website provides education and support for those who are struggling with sex and love addiction. It also provides access to listings of local Sex and Love Addicts Anonymous groups.

Gamblers Anonymous: *www.gamblersanonymous.com*—This website provides education and support for those who have gambling addictions. The website also provides listings of local Gamblers Anonymous meetings.

Anorexic and Bulimics Anonymous: *www.aba12steps.org*—This website provides education and resources for those who are struggling with eating disorders. This website also provides listings of local Anorexic and Bulimic Anonymous groups.

Codependents Anonymous: *www.coda.org*–This website provides resources, support, and education for those who experience patterns of codependency in relationships. This website also provides local listings of Codependent Anonymous groups.

Overeaters Anonymous: *www.oa.org*—This website provides recovery tools, resources, support and education for those who struggle with compulsive overeating, binge eating, or other eating disorders. The website also offers access to a database of local Overeaters Anonymous meetings.

Trauma Survivors Network: *www.traumasurvivorsnetwork.org*—This website provides access to trauma recovery resources and education. The site also provides information about local trauma recovery peer support groups.

Trauma Recovery: EMDR Humanitarian Assistance Program: *trauma-recovery.org*—This program originally began as EMDR Humanitarian Assistance Programs in 1995. It was initially developed in response to the Oklahoma City Bombing and has since expanded to coordinate projects both nationally and internationally. This program coordinates with non-profit companies and inner-city agencies to provide trauma education workshops and clinical trainings for clinicians. The aim of the organization is to prepare clinicians for providing direct services in times of national disasters or emergencies such as acts of terrorism, earthquakes, or humanitarian crises. Although the program is dedicated to providing education and training for clinicians, it can also provide links to direct services upon request.

HelpGuide.org: **Emotional and Psychological Trauma**: *www.helpguide.org/...*
/emotional-and-psychological-trauma-htm.

www.trauma-pages.com: This website provides trauma education and information as well as links for the general public and mental health providers.

US Department of Veterans Affairs: *va.gov*—This organization provides health resources for veterans, including a veterans' crisis line and reading materials on mental health.

Types of Therapy

THE FOLLOWING ARE DESCRIPTIONS of different therapies that are noted to be effective treatment approaches for trauma, PTSD, and related co-occurring disorders. There are many therapeutic approaches that can be effective to reduce trauma symptoms and this list is not mean to exclude additional forms of therapy that haven't been listed. Trauma therapy should be individualized and should address the unique needs of each person. The goal of trauma therapy, regardless of what approach chosen, should be to provide individuals with the safety and structure necessary to process and heal from traumatic events.

Group Therapy—Group therapy is a form of counseling during which a licensed professional counselor or clinical social worker facilitates a group of participants to explore problems, questions, or concerns experienced by individual group members. When group therapy focuses on trauma, group members are provided with opportunities to explore elements of their own traumatic experiences and to receive feedback and support from other group members. Group therapy can help alleviate feelings of loneliness and isolation by allowing members to connect with and provide support for one another in the trauma recovery process.

Individual Therapy—Individual therapy is a form of counseling that involves an individual participant and a licensed mental health professional. Individual therapy allows for in-depth exploration of particular issues or problems. Trauma focused individual therapy allows individuals to move at their own pace to examine specific details related to trauma that they may not be ready to share in a larger group process. Individual therapy can help to process painful feelings and restructure cognitive distortions resulting from traumatic events.

Intensive Outpatient Therapy (IOP)—Intensive Outpatient therapy (IOP), is a six-to-twelve-week structured group counseling program that occurs on an outpatient basis. Group therapy sessions are usually scheduled for nine hours per week. IOP's can address substance use disorders or co-occurring disorders. This type of program might be helpful for individuals with PTSD and co-occurring substance use disorders who require additional support to maintain sobriety.

Inpatient or Residential Treatment—Inpatient or Residential programs provide intensive therapy to individuals who reside at a facility for an extended period of time, usually 30–90 days. These programs usually provide intensive individual and group therapy, medical care, detoxification services, psychiatric care, and specialized treatment interventions. Residential programs often address co-occurring disorders, such as substance use disorders, PTSD, depression, anxiety, nonsuicidal self-injury, sexual addiction, gambling addictions, and mood disorders. Inpatient or Residential treatment programs are useful for individuals who have profound symptoms of depression, anxiety, or have difficulty maintaining sobriety in spite of outpatient treatment attempts. Trauma survivors often benefit from this type of inpatient or residential treatment because it allows them to explore traumatic events and related emotions while in an environment of structure, safety, and support.

SPECIALIZED TREATMENT APPROACHES

Cognitive Behavioral Therapy (CBT)—Cognitive Behavioral Therapy is a form of therapy that addresses negative thoughts and thereby how to reduce associated emotions and behaviors. This approach focuses on the specific problem and works to help clients find solutions. This approach can be useful for trauma survivors who struggle with negative thoughts or beliefs following a traumatic event. CBT can help to improve overall mood by reducing symptoms of PTSD.

Eye Movement Desensitization and Reprocessing Therapy (EMDR)—EMDR is a type of therapy that uses bilateral stimulation (right and left eye movement or tactile stimulation) to activate opposite sides of the brain, thereby releasing painful emotional experiences that are trapped in the brain and nervous system. Research indicates that EMDR is effective in relieving PTSD symptoms and allowing participants to reprocess painful memories and experience alternative emotional experiences such as peace, safety, and acceptance. Although EMDR is an effective and powerful therapeutic tool, it should not be considered for individuals who are psychiatrically unstable. While EMDR can be a form of primary therapy, it is more often used as an adjunct therapy in addition to more traditional counseling approaches.

Mind-Body Therapies—Mind-body therapies are a variety of therapeutic approaches that offer participants an opportunity to make a connection between their brain and body. Trauma survivors often struggle with *depersonalization* and *derealization* as a result of their experiences. Depersonalization can cause an individual to feel disconnected from their own brain and/or body, while derealization can cause an alteration in a person's perceptions about themselves and their surroundings. Both depersonalization and derealization can result from trauma and are a symptom of PTSD. Mind-body therapies provide experiences in which an individual can reconnect with their body or with painful thoughts, feelings, or emotions while remaining present and focused on the here and now. Examples of mind-body therapies include yoga, Chi Nei Tsang, meditation, mindfulness exercises, and tai-chi. These therapies focus on movement, breath, and awareness of body and environment as a means of self-regulation. Mind-body therapies provide participants with an opportunity to develop coping skills to manage painful feelings or thoughts when they arise. These approaches, when used in conjunction with more traditional therapies, can provide relief from symptoms of depression, anxiety, and panic.

Somatic Experiencing (SE)—Somatic Experiencing (SE) is a form of therapy that was introduced in 1997 through Peter Levine's book *Waking the Tiger*. SE addresses symptoms of PTSD and other anxiety and/or panic related disorders. SE proposes that trauma symptoms indicate a dysregulation of the autonomic nervous system. The autonomic nervous system is responsible for helping to regulate emotion and our response to our environment. This therapy involves face-to-face sessions during which participants track painful emotions and physical tension related to past traumatic experiences. SE sessions do not typically focus on discussions of traumatic events, but rather on the bodily sensations, thoughts, and feelings that arise from traumatic memories.

Dialectical Behavior Therapy (DBT)—Dialectical Behavior Therapy (DBT) is a form of cognitive-behavioral therapy that includes four modules: Mindfulness, Distress Tolerance, Emotion Regulation, and Interpersonal Effectiveness. This approach can be useful for individuals with a history of trauma who may struggle with suicidal ideation, self-harm, or other intense trauma symptoms. This approach emphasizes skill-building and countering negative thoughts that result in distressing emotional experiences. While DBT is primarily offered in a group approach, some therapists use skill-building that includes the four modules of DBT.

Narrative Therapy—Narrative therapy is a form of counseling that helps people to examine values, skills, and knowledge and how to use these elements to confront current life problems. This approach focuses on helping people to create or re-create stories about themselves and their identities that may be counter to what they currently believe or think. Narrative therapy asserts that stories about people change their identity or how they view themselves. Trauma survivors can benefit from this approach by recognizing and changing current narratives or stories that they believe about themselves to help them better recognize their strengths and abilities to overcome difficulties.

About the Authors

TANYA LAUER has a master's degree in counseling and psychotherapy and is a Licensed Professional Counselor in Arizona. She has over twenty years' experience working in trauma healing in psychiatric hospitals, in-home therapy services, and outpatient trauma centers. She currently works at Cottonwood Tucson as a trauma specialist and also has a private practice. Tanya has presented at professional conferences in the United States and in Europe. Tanya believes in the importance of healing through the mind body connection.

KATHLEEN PARRISH is a Licensed Professional Counselor in Arizona and the Clinical Director of Cottonwood Tucson, an internationally renowned, residential treatment program for co-occurring disorders in Tucson, Arizona. She has a master's degree in marriage and family therapy, has worked in private practice, and has been involved in providing counseling and trauma intervention services for trauma survivors for over twenty years. She has written for *Counselor, Addiction Professional, Addiction Today* and *Arizona Together* magazines. She has presented seminars on trauma and eating disorders in the United States and Europe.